The Glitter Plan

The Glitter Plan

How We Started Juicy Couture for $200
and Turned It into a Global Brand

PAMELA SKAIST-LEVY
and GELA NASH-TAYLOR
with BOOTH MOORE

GOTHAM BOOKS

GOTHAM BOOKS
Published by the Penguin Group
Penguin Group (USA) LLC
375 Hudson Street
New York, New York 10014

USA | Canada | UK | Ireland | Australia | New Zealand | India | South Africa | China
penguin.com
A Penguin Random House Company

LIBRARY OF CONGRESS CATALOGING-IN-PUBLICATION DATA
has been applied for.

ISBN 978-1-592-40809-2

Printed in the United States of America
10 9 8 7 6 5 4 3 2 1

Set in Adobe Caslon
Designed by Spring Hoteling

To our loving parents, who encouraged us to find our passion and embrace our eccentricity; to our supportive, creative, kick-ass husbands, who stand behind us and let us spend more time together than with them; and to our children, who inspire us every day.

Contents

The Glitter Plan

Chapter 1
The Glitter Plan

This is a fairy tale about two nice girls who like stuff who managed to turn a dream—and $200—into a $1 billion global fashion empire. We also changed the way the world dresses along the way. Not a day goes by that people don't ask us, "How did you do it?" It's one in a million, but it didn't happen overnight. Despite our lack of formal business experience or deep-pocketed family members to bankroll us, we turned a friendship, a love of clothes, and an endless entrepreneurial drive into Juicy Couture.

We didn't just create a brand; we created a whole rainbow-hued Fluffian universe complete with a visual vocabulary (pink power, purse dogs, and matching outfits) and our very own pink Latin, a language we call Juicy speak, with "Smells Like Couture," "Live for Sugar," "Choose Juicy," and other slogans written on T-shirts and across derrieres throughout the land. First was our line of upscale T-shirts in "juicy" colors, buttery fabrics, and curve-hugging fits, then came the velour tracksuit, which turned sweats—once considered full-blown slob wear—into something chic, making them stylish enough to go from carpool to dinner at Mr. Chow.

We put LA style on the map at a time when celebrity was becoming the driving force in fashion. By 2002, when Madonna was photographed wearing velour drawstring pants and a hoodie embroidered with her nickname, "Madge," Juicy had become a full-fledged pop culture phenomenon and the fashion game had changed forever.

Juicy developed a cultish following, too. There are blogs and YouTube videos created by fans who collect our charms, our tracksuits—even our packaging. On Twitter, you can check out @GelaAndPamsArmy. Girls decorate their rooms in our distinctive pink-and-brown color palette and throw Juicy-themed Sweet Sixteen parties. Best friends send us fan letters about how they want to have a brand when they grow up and call it Fruity.

In this book, which is part memoir, part how-to manual, and part fashion industry field guide, we're going to tell you what worked for us for the past twenty-five years (and, for the first time, how the word "couture" became part of our name). The chapters are our stories, our failures, and our successes. And we've listed the lessons learned at the end of each one.

From our honest-to-goodness fairy tale, beginning in the farthest reaches of the San Fernando Valley, to our early days of Dumpster-diving for used denim; from the time we marched into Fred Segal and made our first sale, to the 2003 sale of our company to Liz Claiborne, which netted us more than $200 million, from sitting in the front row at the Paris haute couture shows and on to our next big adventure, we want to share every Juicy detail. And we're going to approach it the way we approached our business: with glitter and guts and stream of thought—and together. We do everything together. We make the first phone call of the day to each other at six thirty A.M. We share not only an intense love of fashion, but an equally intense friendship. We're sisters from another mother, and it's that sisterhood that has guided us.

We never believed in market research. We didn't need twenty people to tell us what was cute or wasn't, or if people were going to like it or not. We had one rule that we keep to this day: We both had to like it. If not, it was out. And, if we both liked it, we knew it was good enough for us. The truth is if you focus on product, create something people want, and find someone in your life who you have the right chemistry with, you can do it, too.

We didn't go to Harvard Business School—or *any* business school—and we never had a business plan. We didn't hire an MBA CEO to run the company—we did this with our own creativity and hard work and often by the seat of our pants. We just wanted to create something people loved and a work environment that made us happy. That's our version of the American Dream.

That's the glitter plan.

Chapter 2
Birds of a Feather

We met in 1988 when we were both working at the Diane Merrick boutique in Los Angeles. It was a classic LA story—we were picking up shifts for a friend who was in rehab. We worked on different days filling in her schedule and everybody thought we were the same person, except that only one of us was helpful (Gela).

Then one afternoon, we were there together, and we bonded while folding the guest towels that went on the sink in the bathroom, of all things. We were both so detail-oriented, we had to make sure every corner on those towels was perfect, even if most people who came into the store were never going to see them.

We definitely both noticed what the other was wearing. Pam was in a straw boater hat from her line Helmet, English riding boots, and black cutoff trouser shorts. Gela was in cowboy boots, kneesocks, and a vintage Victorian children's dress bought at a thrift store. We started gossiping and then got into deeper stuff. It was instant chemistry, like magnets, like we had been friends forever.

Pam: I was born in LA and grew up a skateboarding Valley girl in Encino. I was always outside, climbing trees, riding horses, going to the beach to boogie board, and playing competitive sports, too, but mostly just for the costumes. Encino was a magical sunny place in the 1960s and '70s, a weird melting pot of creative kids who had the burn. The founders of Mossimo, Joie, and True Religion—a crazy Southern California tribe—all grew up there together, and the fashion companies we started grew out of our obsession with SoCal pop culture. My inspiration started with Vans sneakers, Hang Ten T-shirts, and Op shorts. That was California luxury then.

My father, Dr. Leonard Skaist, was a pediatric urologist, and my mom, Elaine, was a homemaker. Both were superpreppy and conservative. When I was a teenager and it came time to shop for back-to-school clothes, my mom tried to take me to Saks and Neiman Marcus in Beverly Hills. But I wanted to go to the surf/skate store Val Surf in the Valley or to Aaardvark's Odd Ark on Melrose Avenue for vintage. When she took me to Aaardvark, she held her nose so she didn't have to smell the stink of old clothes, which made the hunt even more fun for me. I loved that it tortured her.

When it came to style, I had very strong likes and dislikes: After I left the house for school in the morning, I would take my pants off so I could wear my Oingo Boingo T-shirt as a minidress. My mother would say, "Pamela is just expressing herself!"

My younger brother, Mark, and older sister, Lisa, were in all the serious gifted-kid classes in high school. They knew they were going into academia. I knew I wasn't. I loved my friends and I liked lunch. There was one teacher who made me feel passionate about photography and he changed my life. Before that, I knew how to look but I didn't know how to see and edit and form opinions and make creative choices about what I was looking at. I discovered that I loved being able to express myself through an image and it hit me on a visceral level. He gave me the only A I ever got.

When I got older, I put on a great outfit, drove across the hill, and got a job at Fred Segal on Melrose, which was the fashion mecca of Southern California. I worked there on and off for ten years until I got married, including every vacation and school break. I arranged flowers, decorated store windows, and worked in the pit, which is the prime real estate as you walk down the stairs onto the selling floor reserved for the most killer collections. One day, Juicy Couture would own the pit.

After high school, I went to Grossmont College in San Diego, where once more I had an incredible photography teacher, and I put all of my focus on that class. But I still didn't know what I wanted to do with my life. After college, I moved back to LA and into a house with my friends, where we spent all night partying and all day sleeping. Eventually, my parents made me get it together, and I decided to apply to the Fashion Institute of Design and Merchandising in Los Angeles.

On the first day of FIDM in 1985, the teacher asked the class, "What is the job of a designer?" Some people said, "To make patterns." Others said, "To be creative." But the right answer was this: The job of a designer is to solve problems. And that is a big lesson. Every day when you are running a business, there is a problem to solve.

For an independent study, I launched a line of hats named Helmet and sold them at Fred Segal. Once my hats were selling there, getting them into Barneys New York and Neiman Marcus was easy. (That's how much weight Fred Segal carried at the time.) My senior project was to design a whole clothing collection, and I was the only one in the class who did down-to-earth T-shirts and casual clothes, as opposed to fanciful paper or tinfoil ball gowns. My teacher told me that I knew how to build a collection. I realized that I didn't have to be good at everything; I just had to focus on what moved me.

While I was going to FIDM, I was also working as a waitress at Sushi On Sunset, where I met my future husband, producer-director Jefery Levy. We were wearing the same round tortoise-and-wire nerd glasses. (I said to him, "I like your glasses," and he said to me, "I like your face." We have been together ever since.) Jef was wearing the coolest Yohji Yamamoto trench coat and hanging out with the Brat Pack. It was a lightning-bolt moment; he was an artist wearing cool clothes and making it. I wanted to be part of that.

I started designing clothes for a vampire film called *Rockula,* which Jef wrote—I just put in clothes that I loved: cameo necklaces and riding jackets that I sewed bits of lace onto. I even hand-painted suits. I didn't know I needed duplicates of costumes, and I made everything one-of-a-kind. We were filming an action scene, and Thomas Dolby ripped his jacket by mistake. They said, "Send in the stunt suit!" and I'm like, "Stunt suit?! What's that?!"

I liked designing costumes up to a point, but when yelling and budgets and dealing with jerky action film producers came into play, I didn't like it so much. The last film I did starred George Clooney. Being a prankster, I did make continuity blunders on purpose because I knew I was out of there. I was ready for something new. Then I met Gela.

Gela: I was born in Corning, New York. My family moved to a new state every three years or so, which was an excellent opportunity to reinvent my style. Always being the new girl in a new school was also a recipe for an overly active, insanely glamorous imagination.

My dad, Edwin, was an executive at several big steel corporations. Business was his passion, and he never dressed down. In fact, there was nothing casual about him. He read six newspapers a day and when friends came over on the weekends, we had to be quiet so we didn't disturb him. But he was a great mentor.

My mother, Sara, on the other hand, was an exotic bird in those small towns. She was obsessed with clothes, whether it was Koos Van Den Akker or the little white muslin dresses she used to buy and embroider herself. I remember my mother getting stopped in the elevator one time and someone asking for her autograph. She just looked like somebody.

I had a flair for the dramatic, too. My childhood nickname was Miss Priss the Hollywood Miss. For me, clothes were—and are still—a second skin. Just like when an actress puts on a corset in a period play, it alters her persona, if you are wearing a hat or a fur or a certain color, it changes the way you feel and act.

I remember my life by what I wore. I started wearing heels when I was around five years old, these plastic glitter heels that made the best *click-clack*ing sound ever. Middle school was ultraproblematic as I was weirdly petite—crazy short and insanely skinny. My mother used to take me to the doctor for worm tests to try and understand the reason for my glaring size discrepancy. I wanted to wear tight pencil skirts, but the only clothes that fit me were kids' clothes—all white and cutesy with tiny ducks. So I often had to improvise.

As a teenager, I was all about hippie-chic fringe jackets, Landlubber hip-hugging jeans, floppy hats, granny dresses, and Indian jewelry. I loved Jimi Hendrix (those white go-go boots!) and Anita Pallenberg, the Rolling Stones, and the whole 1970s look. I also had a bit of a penchant for pure shock-value dressing. In 1972, much to my mother's horror, I went to the interview for my uptight all-girls boarding school, Stoneleigh-Burnham in Greenfield, Massachusetts, in a see-through organza blouse. And, shockingly, I got accepted.

In high school, I got serious about acting. I auditioned and was accepted to the most top-of-the line acting school, Carnegie Mellon. When I told my parents I was accepted and was going to Carnegie Mellon to study acting, that didn't count in their world. It was like I was going to summer camp. My older sister, Anita, went to Columbia and got an MBA, and my younger sister, Carol, became a nurse practitioner.

After graduating in 1978, I moved to New York City to be an actress. I was roommates with Cherry Jones and Diane Sutherland, and we were all trying to make it. I appeared on Broadway in *Zoot Suit*. In the early 1980s, I moved to LA to try to find TV work. In between auditioning for acting gigs (I appeared on *Hill Street Blues* and *Taxi*), I got a job working at the Azzedine Alaïa boutique on Rodeo Drive. I had no retail experience, but was so obsessed with him as a designer, I just had to work there (and have the clothes; it was all about the clothes). I also met and married my first husband, Chris Nash, a musician and actor.

At the time, Peter Morton's girlfriend, Tarlton Pauley, was working at Alaïa, too. When I joined them for dinners, all Tarlton wanted to talk about was shopping. But I wanted to make money, not spend it. I was more interested in Peter's business, the Hard Rock Café. He bought memorabilia at auction to put in the stores, and manufactured souvenirs, T-shirts, cups, and mugs to sell there. How had he created a world that seemed like it had been around forever? It was his obsession with having the perfect American hamburger while he was living in London, and his love of rock 'n' roll, he told me.

It was the first brand I noticed that had been invented out of thin air. When the Hard Rock Café opened in LA, everyone wanted to go there. It was a very cool place with a velvet rope outside. Then he spun off the idea into the Hard Rock Hotel in Vegas, the first young, hip place there. He helped change the reputation of Vegas as old and stodgy to cool and hip.

Peter Morton was a beacon, he was my entrepreneurial idol. And his stories got the wheels turning in my head. I was getting disillusioned with acting. I was talented but I didn't have the commercial, all-American look—that's what producers and casting directors told me. There was so much waiting around, too—for auditions, callbacks. I was a doer. I wanted to be in control of my life. And if I wasn't going to win an Oscar, I wasn't interested. Whenever I thought of anything I wanted to do, if it was acting or going into business, I only thought of it in the biggest way possible. And if I couldn't get to that level of success, I was going to move on.

Then I met Pam.

That day folding towels at Diane Merrick, we discovered that we had a lot in common. We were both the daughters of workaholic fathers who were probably the world's only Jewish Republicans. Gela's first charm bracelet had a heart-shaped "Nixon" charm, and we both cried when Nixon was impeached. We didn't know why, we just cried because we knew our fathers would be sad. We were both middle children (which we believe is one of the driving forces behind our success) and the black sheep of our families. One of us spent our childhood being dragged around the great U.S.A., and one of us was born and bred in LA and never dragged out, but when we met, we were at similar times of our lives, trying to figure out what was next.

The trick to our success—and any success—is passion; you can't manufacture that. You have to find that one thing you love more than anything. And for both of us, it was fashion: That was our biggest connection. We both had loved clothes for as long as we could remember. We were the costume dressers in our families, the eccentric freak-a-zoids. We were cuckoo for clothes, and not just fur or couture. It could be a vintage pair of pajamas from Jet Rag. Whatever it was, we loved it.

Gela had mentioned to a mutual friend of ours named Blair that she had an idea to make maternity jeans. Since Pam had gone to fashion school and already started her own line of hats, Blair suggested we get together on the jeans idea. Now, most partnerships end with one person walking out the door. But we didn't know that at the time, and we thought, Why not? We can have fun together. We were in the same universe, had friends in common, and liked each other's style.

So one afternoon, we went on a research expedition to some of the maternity stores in Beverly Hills, and we were aghast at how shockingly ugly the clothes were. We knew we could do better. And that day, our partnership was born. In a good partnership, it's not like you say one person is going to do this, and the other this. There wasn't a division of labor like that. It was more symbiotic. And we never for a split second thought about doing it any other way than fifty-fifty.

As an entrepreneur, finding the right partner gives you the opportunity to experience crazy things, and you've got someone to hug and cry and scream and laugh and love. It's the same thing as any great relationship. You have a partner in crime through everything—good, bad, or ugly, here we are. Everything is better with two, whether you are moving in unison or one is pulling the other along.

Before you go into business with somebody, you have to be an archaeologist. Dig in there and investigate if it's the right person or not. For us, it was intuition. We knew we were birds of a feather. So many partnerships fall apart because you get started and then realize you don't see eye to eye. You have to find a like-minded person, somebody who you like to play in the sandbox with. You spend more time with a business partner than almost anyone. You don't need to have the same creative vision all the time, but you do need the same values and ethics. It's like a marriage. It's through sickness and health. When things go well and you're happy, of course you love each other. But when things don't turn out how you expect, can you weather the storm together?

When it came to setting up our work environment, we agreed we didn't want anything remotely like a traditional office setting. We learned something very important from our fathers: We didn't want to be in an office until eleven P.M. We wanted work to be fun and loose. There is no security in corporate life anymore, so you might as well do what makes you happy. We didn't want a separation between life and work, because what you do is who you are. And when you work in a great environment, you get so much more done in a minute. The more you enjoy your work, the better business is going to be. Your product is going to be great, and the customer experience is going to be great. If you are passionate and engaged, you are going to want to get it right and you're not going to be wasting time. And having a partner who feels the same way will make the ride that much more enjoyable.

You have to set up an environment that is inspiring and true to you. Although we didn't think about it at the time, we took a holistic approach that's the opposite of how most corporate jobs are set up today. Ours was the female way, not the stodgy-old-boys'-club way. What we did was organic to us, what was necessary at the time, and it worked. And it is why so many women are starting their own businesses now, because the old way doesn't reflect the complexity of women's lives. No, we can't all build personal nurseries next to our offices like (Yahoo! CEO) Marissa Mayer. No one had to tell us to "lean in," but we did need to keep things fluid and do things in a way that worked for us.

We set up our offices home-style in Gela's one-bedroom Hollywood apartment on Spaulding Avenue, and sat around the kitchen table. And because we were friends, it was never hard to go to work. We solved a big problem that women have in the workplace—affordable, reliable child care—by bringing our kids to work with us. And it was fun having them there jumping in and out of the boxes on the living room floor. We kept the hours flexible, too. We've always believed if you get in there and you really get it done, you don't need to stay until midnight. You have to be self-motivated to be an entrepreneur.

As we said earlier, we never had a business plan—not an MBA type of business plan, anyway. We each put in $100 and that money went straight into the product. We started small, with one specific item, and set out to see if there was a market for it. Our approach to financing was definitely from a woman's perspective. We could only do it like housewives—we're spending this, and we won't do that until we make that money back. We borrowed and paid it back, borrowed and paid it back.

We had the freedom of mind to think like mavericks,

which is another key to being an entrepreneur. But we also had an understanding of the commerce side. A lot of bohemian people can't pull it together on the commerce side. And sometimes we don't like to admit we have that commerce side, but we do. If you're not making money, it's not a real business; it's a hobby. If it's a business, you're profitable.

For us, it wasn't about formal titles and a strict delegation of responsibilities, like Gela was responsible for the business side and Pam the creative side, for example. We both did it all. We didn't speak the language of business, but we were intuitive marketers and merchandisers. To be an entrepreneur, you have to be able to improvise and to make decisions fast. Do what moves you. And as you get bigger, you will learn that you can hire what you don't know.

When we started, there were no cell phones, no BlackBerrys. We hand wrote our invoices. We packed our own boxes. We drove our own delivery van. We had to learn every aspect of our industry the hard way: factoring and manufacturing, what a SKU is and what a style is. But we also had a blast. And fun became part of our aesthetic.

Our parents called us the baby mogulettes. They said, "How on earth did you two find each other?" We don't know, but thank God we did. We both trust people, which is a nutty thing. And we've always trusted each other. Weirdly, our little fairy tale seems so simple now, mainly because we had no idea of what lay ahead. As they say, ignorance is bliss. Now close your eyes and let us take you back to the very beginning.

Do What Moves You and Find Your Partner in Crime

Believe in yourself first or no one else will.

We were cuckoo for clothes. When thinking about what kind of business you want to start, make it your passion—that one thing you're so obsessed with, you can't help but do it 24/7.

Before you go into business with a partner, be an archaeologist and dig deep. Is this someone you trust AND want to do tequila shots with? Make sure you have a like-minded vision and enjoy each other's company.

Set up an office that feels like home, a safe, loving place to create that's filled with dogs and candy and inspiration.

Working for yourself is supposed to be fun, but don't forget you're in it to make money. If you don't, you've got a hobby, not a business.

Think like a maverick but budget like a housewife. Borrow if you must, but pay it back as fast as you can.

Chapter 3

A Shortfall in Shortalls

Every brand has an origin story. Some start at a Vegas poker table, others in a Silicon Valley garage. Ours started in the courtyard of an apartment building, drying freshly washed maternity jeans under the California sun. When we first went into business together in 1988, we decided to take on the very unglamorous world of maternity wear. Our company was called Travis Jeans for the Baby in You, after Gela's son, who was born that year. And although it wasn't crazily profitable, it turned out to be a brilliant little niche market to learn our craft. It really was our business school. Sourcing, manufacturing, production, marketing, returns, defects—we learned it all as we went along. And we were invisible to a certain extent, so we could mess up without the whole fashion world watching.

We have always believed that we have to be our own customers. In other words, unless it is something we would wear, we won't make it. When Gela was pregnant, there wasn't anything in the maternity department she would have touched with a ten-foot pole. It all looked like something from the *I Love Lucy* era: oversize like a tent. So she improvised. She cut up a pair of her husband's vintage Levi's jeans and sewed in a Lycra band where the waistband should be. She wore those superfaded ripped jeans with holes in the knees, and little white cotton-and-lace Victorian tops, and people looked at her in disbelief. "How in the hell are you pregnant and still wearing those cool old Levi's?" they asked. No one could even tell there was a soft, expandable Lycra panel sewn underneath. The jeans looked like clothes we would wear whether we were pregnant or not.

It was a very specific, targeted idea, which is the best way to start something. So, after some inspiration from the film *Baby Boom*, in which Diane Keaton basically says, "Take this corporate job and shove it," moves to Vermont, and starts her own couture applesauce business, we decided to go for it. Gela had the goods, and Pam had already made a name for herself in the fashion business with her line of hats. But before we spent any serious cash, or borrowed any money, we needed to make sure other people liked our idea as much as we did. So we agreed to go in fifty-fifty and spend $100 each to make some jeans.

We drove to a rag house, which is a wholesale retailer of used clothing sold by the pound. We pulled up to this place in a god-awful industrial section of LA and it was like we had died and gone to heaven. Imagine a warehouse filled with mountains of used denim, taller than the two of us put together. It was shopping nirvana! It did not smell like couture, but we didn't care. We jumped in with our tape measures, picked through all the stinky jeans, and measured each pair to find the ones that would work for sizes XS, S, M, L, and XL. There was no Purell-ing. We were filthy. And we laughed about how our highly educated sisters with MBAs and law degrees would have hated it. Listen up, entrepreneurs: Get down, get dirty, or get out!

We took the jeans directly to the Laundromat because they were beyond nasty. Then we brought them home to dry outside in the LA sun. We covered the entire courtyard of Gela's *Melrose Place*–style apartment building with the jeans. Once they were dry, we cut out the waistbands using special scissors that cut through denim, and man, our hands got sore. But we were loving crafting! We found a sample sewer through Gela's sister Anita (who had a bicycle clothing company called Alitta) and had her sew on the Lycra panels. The hardest thing for entrepreneurs is to figure out how to get started. But the first step forward is easier than you think. You don't need to worry about hiring someone full-time; you can find someone freelance to do the work, or even ask an alterations shop to sew something up. Always try to do it the easy way and the most economical way first.

We needed a label, so we went to our local fabric shop, International Silk & Woolens, the same place we bought the Lycra panels, and found a couple yards of pale blue iron-on polka-dot fabric. We cut the iron-on fabric into strips with pinking shears. And those strips became our labels. On each one, we wrote with a Sharpie pen, "Travis Jeans for the Baby in You." It was pretty lo-fi, but we did it the way we could do it. We didn't say, "We need fifteen thousand dollars to go downtown to a factory that makes fancy labels." It was a DIY punk-rock mentality.

If you have an idea, figure out how to make it in the least expensive way possible. Then find a local store that has strong relationships with customers—there's one in every town—go to the store and see if they like your product. If they are into it, they will showcase it and your product will get out there through word of mouth. Or put it online or on your blog. You have to work it.

Our first stop was Diane Merrick, the boutique where we were both working when we met. Our friend Tracey Ross, who was the top salesperson there at the time, freaked out when she saw our funky one-of-a-kind jeans with different washes. "Oh my God, I can totally sell those!" she said. Tracey is a part of LA's fashion-culture history. She was a phenomenon in bringing the worlds of celebrity and fashion together, the first person to really cultivate a celebrity clientele that she could call on and send boxes of clothes to. Her access was a powerful tool that helped many fashion brands gain exposure in Hollywood and beyond, including ours. When she saw our cool maternity jeans, she knew five people who were pregnant and one of them was Melanie Griffith.

Thanks to Tracey, we lucked out early on with a piece of press, a little story in *Glamour* magazine that asked the question, "What do Melanie Griffith and the singer Pebbles have in common?" It was our jeans. And it was super-exciting. People were blown away by the photos. They said we were revolutionizing maternity wear. And in a sense we were, bringing real clothes to a world that had been all pussy bows and polka dots. There was this crazy rule in the maternity world that the front of a garment has to be three inches longer than the back. We hated that. The whole industry was stuck in the 1950s. Now, every fashion brand under the sun has maternity jeans, from J Brand to Juicy. We brought normal fashion to maternity, and helped move the needle.

We took samples of the jeans all around town, carrying them from place to place in the trunk of our car. The maternity world was so dead ugly at the time, people wanted to buy these jeans on the spot. Fred Segal, which was our backyard store, put them in the pit. They were priced at $89 each, which was a lot of money, but people bought them. We would always have loyalty to Fred Segal. Ron Herman and John Eshaya weren't just buyers; they were the coolio arbiters of taste in LA. If they gave you the thumbs-up, you were golden. We also took the jeans into A Pea in the Pod and Mother's Work, which were the biggest maternity chains at the time. We just barged our funky selves into the stores on Ventura Boulevard, went into the fitting room, and tried on the jeans with pregnancy pillows. We gave the sales staff a little show, and it worked. They called their buyers and placed orders. We didn't know you weren't supposed to cold-call stores or bust in and show the salespeople stuff. One of our favorite mottos has always been this: "The question isn't who's going to let me, it's who's going to stop me." We believe that. If something is good enough, they'll want to see it. It's all about product. It always has been and it always will be.

We packed the store orders ourselves using black electrical tape to seal the boxes because that's all we had. We put a sprig of dried lavender (which probably crumbled all over everything) inside every one, and a thank-you note saying, "We hope you love our product." We did what we liked, and never got stopped by someone saying, "Oh no, someone could be allergic to those flowers." It was all about keeping it personal—something from us to the customer. We've always said we really believe if something is made with love, if it's made in an authentic, caring way, people will respond. We have always been hands-on, and people look for that quality in clothes. They don't want anything too corporate or mass. We had people all along saying, "You're not big enough. You're never going to ship enough to succeed." What we did in the beginning was go around all those people. We just kept doing it any way we could until we got big enough, and then we found a factory to make our labels—and our jeans. You don't have to invest thousands. You can do it our way, grassroots style.

As orders picked up, we started to have a lot of shipments going out of that tiny little apartment. We were around the corner from Fairfax Senior High School, so we asked one of the students if he wanted to help us move boxes from the second-floor apartment to the street. We offered him $20 an hour, and he wouldn't do it! He said it wasn't enough. We ended up carrying all the stuff ourselves, but we couldn't believe that. How did he know it wouldn't turn into a full-time job? You have to start somewhere, and you can't be afraid to get your hands dirty.

When it came to building brand awareness, we knew the product was cool, but maternity was not cool. So we decided to shake things up. And because we did not have a lot of resources for marketing or advertising, we relied on our friends, just like Lana Del Rey did when she tapped her friends to shoot her first video, rather than spending thousands of dollars for a slick videographer. Gen Y-ers know all about that. They always use their friends. And we believe that they are on the forefront of what is a real entrepreneurial moment. This is the first generation to graduate from school and not go into corporate life.

After we were selling to a few stores, we got a wholesale license and decided to take our jeans to a maternity trade show in Dallas attended by store buyers from all over the Southwest and West. We wanted some visuals to be able to display in our exhibition booth (along with a jar of Hershey's Kisses, because everything is better with candy). Sandra Bernhard was in a movie Pam's husband was directing, *Inside Monkey Zetterland*, and she had become a friend. It got us thinking about how hysterical it would be to have her model in our maternity campaign. We had seen her in *Kings of Comedy* and thought she was the funniest goddamn person ever. We loved her, and we loved her style. Turns out, Sandra thought it was pretty hysterical, too, and agreed to do it.

The plan was to make Sandra look like Brigitte Bardot, to spoof the famous 1985 Guess Jeans ad campaign with Claudia Schiffer. We hired Davis Factor, another friend, who was just starting out as a photographer, to take the pictures in black-and-white. We put Sandra in a sexy Bardot blonde wig. She was topless, holding her boobs, and pursing her killer lips, wearing our jeans with a pregnancy pillow underneath. It was genius! Our tagline? "Red Hot Mama." You don't have to follow the rules when it comes to marketing and brand building. Our strategy has always been to think outside the box. When we do that, it usually strikes a chord and other people like it, too. But if we had told anyone in the traditional marketing world that we were going to use Sandra Bernhard as a pregnancy model with a pillow, they would have told us we were crazy. But she was our girl, a maverick. We've always had a sense of humor—with Travis Jeans, Juicy, and beyond.

At the maternity trade show, everyone was obsessed with the photos, which we had made into life-size posters, including the buyers from A Pea in the Pod. They thought we were going to breathe fresh air into the business, and asked us to design an exclusive line for the chain. Obviously, we knew a thing or two about marketing. We were pushing the envelope. And it wasn't the last time.

When we got big enough to start having our labels made in a factory, we thought it would be funny to have a photo of baby Travis on each one. We wanted to give him an edgy look, so we took him to Hollywood Boulevard to get a temporary tattoo put on his arm. It was a heart with the word "Mom" written inside. He wore a diaper and a black leather biker cap. After the pictures were taken, we took Travis to a party at Diane Merrick's store, and she started yelling, "Are you crazy?" She thought we had really gotten him tattooed. We were becoming the enfants terribles of the maternity world, which was just what it needed at the time because it was so uptight and dull.

We went from having a freelance sample sewer sewing up ten pairs at a time, to finding factories downtown to sew up batches of fifty to one hundred pairs of jeans using the denim we picked at the rag house, to buying denim by the yard, making a pattern, and creating thousands of pairs of jeans with a vintage look by working with a denim wash house. That's how a business grows organically. The need becomes so great that you have to figure out a way to produce more. We had to do our research to find resources for fabric, trim, and labels, as well as the factories that worked with denim and the factors who loaned money. So we consulted the TALA, or Textile Association of Los Angeles, directory. There is something like it for every industry, and now every directory is online.

For quite a while, we were self-financed. But eventually, we needed more cash flow. A good rule of thumb is if you can borrow from your family, do it. If you can't, go to an apparel factor. We did both. We asked our parents to cosign for a $75,000 revolving line of credit, and we also used a factor, who loaned us money based on the value of our orders from stores. What factors do is brilliant, because they credit check the boutiques you are selling to, and won't ship to stores that don't have good credit. So you get an extra service and extra protection. Of course, you pay for it with high interest rates. But they do a lot of the back-office stuff that's useful for young entrepreneurs who don't have their own accounting departments. When we got orders, we borrowed money to buy our fabric. Then when the stores paid us, we paid down our debt. As we got better and better about paying it back, the factors and the banks loaned us more.

One of myths is that people think we had all this money and it was never hard for us. Gela got divorced in 1991. After that, she was a single mother with two kids. (Zoe was born in 1990.) Work was the motivator that helped her through that rough time. There were many moments of living from month to month, however, it was comforting to feel like we were in control of our own destinies. We have always been firm believers that we are captains of our own ship, and that we are in charge of our lives. Neither of us are into just sitting at home, waiting for someone to call or something to happen, and hoping, hoping.

A friend gave us a good piece of advice early on, and told us we had to start taking a salary. "It doesn't matter if you pay yourself a thousand dollars or a hundred dollars," she said. "If you don't start paying yourself you're never going to think of this as a business." She was right about that. Our first paycheck was $2,000 apiece. It had to last us about six months. It wasn't a lot, but it was what we could afford. We were still putting most of our money back into the business. But we did start paying ourselves and slowly started paying ourselves more, until we got to a whopping $27,000 a year each at Juicy. We always paid ourselves less than anyone who worked for us. We always bonused our employees before we ever gave ourselves a bonus. That's a healthy way to run a start-up business.

We had some hilarious times when we were baby entrepreneurs. When it came time to pick up a batch or "cut" of clothing, we'd rent a huge white monster van and head downtown to the factory. One beautiful sunny day, we went to pick up a cut of shortalls for A Pea in the Pod. Shortalls, if you don't know, are overall shorts, which is a hideous visual, but was a 1990s fashion thing. So there we were in this van with one thousand pairs of shortalls in the back, laughing and talking, cranking up the radio and singing "Los Angeles" by X at the top of our lungs. We made a pit stop for candy and Slurpees at 7-Eleven, as we often do, and something looked strange about the van. We went to the back to check out our booty . . . and no shortalls. We started laughing so hard we were throwing up. How could we have been talking and singing so loud that somebody at a stoplight could steal a thousand pairs of shortalls without us even noticing? We called our buyer at A Pea in the Pod and said, "We've got good news and bad news. The cut of shortalls looked pretty good. The bad news is they're all gone." Most people would have flipped out after having lost a thousand pieces. But we took it in stride. And we still managed to have fun.

By the early 1990s, we had a full line of maternity wear, including denim shirts and blazers, riding pants and catsuits, which we always fit on ourselves. We were always looking for new product extensions. It's a natural part of who we are and what we do well. We feel like a fashion cycle is three years, then you have to roll out something new. You have to keep evolving. One of our product extensions was a big success (denim diaper bags). Another was not.

We launched a line of nursing bras called Foundations, which ended up being a total loser fest. Maternity nursing bras were deadly at the time, and we wanted to make lacy, pretty ones. Little did we know that making bras is complicated stuff. There were tons of moving parts. Each bra had twenty-six components—hooks, underwires, rings—not to mention all the band and cup sizes you have to make. We needed help. So we hired a production manager. We thought she would be able to keep us superorganized, and were excited to employ someone who we thought was a real professional. But this was a major lesson for us about hiring. She mystified us. She was like a character out of a Dickens novel. All day, all she seemed to do was sit with a tiny scale, weighing each little hook and ring by the hundreds, counting out how many we had. Spying her through the doorway we asked ourselves, "Why are we paying her three hundred dollars a day to do that? We could do that." She had to go.

We learned early on to make sure the people we were able to employ fit into our culture, and that they understood our speak and believed our dream. Don't just go off a résumé. In the end, our misguided, mystifying, would-be production manager couldn't have helped us anyway. Bras were just too complex for our infrastructure. You have to figure out how complicated a product is going to be to make, the minimums on orders for the components, and how much capital you need to put in beforehand. It may not be worth it. We stopped making the bras, but that didn't mean we stopped paying for them. We have always had good relationships with our suppliers and kept our word and commitments. We spent years paying off the $12,000 we owed Klauber Brothers, Inc., Lace and Embroiderers. Our last check to them was $11.25. The woman from the collections department was truly impressed. "I never thought a vendor would do that, but you were honorable," she told us. And that felt good. It goes back to our values, and it's why we make great partners. We both believe you have to keep it real, and relate to the people you are buying from and selling to. It sounds elementary, but it's the truth. Make it with love and your customer feels it. That's the only way to do it.

Anything you need to know in a bigger pond we learned in a smaller pond. We learned about the importance of quality control from teachers who helped us understand that when a production error occurred, like an armhole being seriously off spec, we had to send it back to the factory. We just had to. And we learned not to freak out. It's part of doing business. Over the years, we also got to know some wonderful contractors in downtown LA's garment district. One of them literally saved our business in 1992 during the LA riots. It was a scary time in Los Angeles. There was a curfew, and the police advised everyone to stay home with their curtains closed. We had so much denim in production downtown, that if it had been lost, Travis Jeans would have been over. When the riots were stopped and the curfews lifted, we raced downtown. It was a wasteland. There were no cars, no people. You could still see smoldering buildings. It was like a war zone. A lot of factories had burned down. But ours was safe because the Korean owners were hardcore. They had been on the roof of the factory defending it with machine guns.

After the riots, we didn't want to be driving downtown all the time, two girls on their own, to go to factories and dye houses. At the same time, we were quickly outgrowing Gela's apartment. So we started looking for office and production spaces elsewhere. Our crazy friend Bruce, an ultra-preppy guy who had a line of nursing T-shirts he wore himself to demonstrate how the flaps lifted, suggested we check out the place where he worked, the Golden State Business Park in Pacoima. We loved it, and moved in. Pacoima has to be one of the least chic parts of Southern California. It's a chop shop area for sure, and it seemed like there was always a burned-out, stripped-down car in the alley, but having our headquarters in Pacoima became part of our story that lasted through the Juicy years. We did our design, production, and shipping from the same spot. Of course, not long after we moved, the Northridge earthquake hit in 1994, which was another scare. For several days we didn't know if our warehouse was totaled and cordoned off behind yellow caution tape, or if we were still in business. It wasn't until Bruce, who was a part-time danger junkie and now our neighbor in the business park, reported back to us from the hot zone. He had gone by our tiny office in Unit G, looked in the windows, and now gave us the all clear.

We were rolling along, steadily making our maternity clothes, selling them all over the country and internationally to multiple retail stores. And things were going pretty well—until they weren't. We had been feeling for some time an itch to begin making "real" clothes—by that we mean nonmaternity clothes that we could both wear. Neither of us was pregnant and we just couldn't relate to that world anymore. We were starting to realize the limitations of our little niche market. Something happened in 1994 that was the last straw. We had designed a spring collection for A Pea in the Pod that was gingham-checked—yes, for a pregnant person—including a catsuit, skirt, and jacket. The collection was red, white, and blue, which has always been one of our favorite color stories. But A Pea in the Pod did some market research, and decided to change the color scheme from red, white, and blue to the ugliest bright orange, yellow, and lime green. In their hands, the look was Hot Dog on a Stick all the way. At the factory, Gela tried to pretend the stuff wasn't ours. We were sure the collection was going to bomb. But it turned out to have the highest sell-through of anything we had ever done for them. It was a major success. But how? We wanted to make a documentary film and travel the country to see who the hell was wearing those clothes! There is a lesson to be learned from that, too: that you don't always know what is going to hit with people. But for us, this was a question of taste.

When we saw each other after we heard the news, we looked at each other and said, "We have to get out." If that heinous Hot Dog on a Stick collection was selling, we knew we had no idea what we were doing. We no longer had a feel for what was good and bad in the maternity market. We could have been making all the money in world, but if the passion was gone, who cared? After that, we realized our days designing maternity wear were numbered. We were over it. We wanted to do things that were tighter and more fitted. We had a vision and a style that was forever—not just for nine months.

In the end, we traded our Travis Jeans patterns to Bruce for a color copy machine. And it turned out that copy machine didn't even work.

As an entrepreneur, you have to love what you do, but that doesn't mean every business you do is going to be a success. Not everything works. The maternity world was the perfect way for us to start. We didn't jump onto the freeway going seventy miles an hour. We were just on our bicycles going along. But we never thought it would be a forever business. We were both dying to get into contemporary ready-to-wear, and we were now ready. We knew we had to make what we were into. If we weren't excited by the product, ultimately our customers wouldn't be, either. But we didn't even think about not continuing together.

Learn from a Starter Business

Before Juicy, we started a maternity wear line called Travis Jeans. It wasn't crazily profitable, but it ended up being our equivalent of business school—an opportunity to learn our craft in a niche market, where we could experiment, mess up, and stay hidden from the rest of the fashion industry. We learned production, marketing, sourcing, and more, but most of all, we learned the rules that young entrepreneurs should live by:

You have to be your own customer. If you won't buy it, who will?

Be prepared to go Dumpster-diving for resources. In other words, get down, get dirty, or get out.

Don't wait for big bucks to come along; have a DIY punk-rock mentality.

If you have an idea, don't go begging and borrowing. Always try to do it the easiest (and cheapest) way first to see if it flies.

Find a testing ground. Get your product into the hands of local shop owners, friends, and mentors, and listen to their feedback to refine the product. But also listen to your gut.

Be the enfants terribles of your world. In other words, shake things up and people will notice.

Start paying yourself a salary as soon as you can. It will help you take your business more seriously.

Don't go off résumés; hire people who fit your culture (or in our case, have a good haircut).

Not every business is going to be a success, but that doesn't mean you don't learn from it. Pick up and move on to the next one with even more focus on what you want.

Chapter 4

Dying for the Perfect T-shirt

After we decided to get out of the maternity business, there was no looking back. We're not depressos. We're fighters and optimists. And we were ready to get into the big leagues. We glorified that casual, easy California lifestyle and wanted to dress the world, starting with the perfect, well-fitting, buttery-soft T-shirt in amazing colors. And that's how Juicy was born in 1994.

Naming is important, whether you're naming a kid, a band, or a brand. A lot of businesses spend a fortune researching names and do focus groups to find out if names will strike a chord with people. We weren't like that; we were instinctual. So we had a huge brainstorming session and batted around hundreds of ideas. We talked about using Revolution, which would have been a kick-ass name in an Exene Cervenka kind of way, and Uniform, which reminded us of Pam's hat company, Helmet. We even thought about Valley, because the San Fernando Valley was where our offices were. But none of those names were right for the casual luxury lifestyle we were going for. They didn't evoke Cali, fun, and sun. Then we hit on the name Juicy (Couture came later) and it felt right in our gut. It was not some sly sexual reference as some people thought, because there's nothing like that about the two of us. We just thought it was a cute, colorful, sunny name. And although we didn't know it at the time, it turned out to be a great branding name that could be tagged onto a million products. But it all started with a T-shirt.

If you're considering starting a business, think about this: You are the customer. Do you want it, meaning the product you're making? We have always approached design in a practical sense, which is different from some other designers. For us, it's about what we want to wear every day, and what we can't find but need in our own closets. We are the customers.

Today, there are a ton of T-shirt companies out there. But these were the days before T-shirts were a real fashion category, and before brands like Ella Moss, Splendid, and James Perse had come on the scene. Michael Stars and Tease Tees were the only games in town. Michael Stars made T-shirts that were boxy and oversize, and Tease Tees made cropped baby tees with crew necks. But there was room for plenty more. We wanted a designer-quality, body-conscious, buttery-soft T-shirt that through fabrication would not lose its shape—something that would appeal to young and old and be so yummy that you had to have it in every Juicy color.

When it came to making the perfect T-shirt, the starting point was our own wardrobe. We used to buy Hanes T-shirts in packages of three at the Target next to our office in Pacoima, but wouldn't wear them before cutting them up, altering them, and making them fit better. Because we are both petite, we were used to altering our clothing by taking it to Crown Cleaners on Fairfax, or the Hemster on Laurel Canyon. That was life. And it was an advantage that put us in the mind-set of knowing what we liked and didn't like about the way something fits. Hanes V-necks were okay, but they were designed for men, which meant they were superboxy and not flattering. They didn't have the perfect V-neck, either, and the fabric wasn't luxe.

When you're starting out, you have to find your DNA. We wanted to improve on that T-shirt, to give it a better fit, fabric, and color. Although we didn't know it at the time, fit, fabric, and color was our brand DNA. It became business speak that we used in our marketing to describe our guiding principles for creating casual luxury basics that make your body look insane.

We looked for the fabric first. We had something in mind reminiscent of the 1970s-era, French-style T-shirts we grew up wearing from a line called Tea by Nancy Heller. They were popular with our childhood style icons Dinah Shore, Angie Dickinson, Lindsay Wagner, and Farrah Fawcett. They were the crazy ultimate. To try to re-create that, we needed fabric that really hugged your body and stayed there. It couldn't be too heavy. It couldn't be too thin. The shirts had to have return, meaning that if you washed them twenty-five times, they didn't get stretched out and they stayed soft and got better over time. They also had to take dye in a gorgeous way.

It wasn't going to be easy to find all that. When we started the company, it was a recession and price was everything. But what we wanted was the highest-quality combed cotton. That was the cutting-edge technology then. If it was carded, it was very crunchy and stiff, like something you buy at a souvenir shop. (Think cardboard.) Combed was beautiful, luxurious, fine-combed yarn. While we're at it, a few notes on some other technical terms we learned during our early days in the T-shirt business. Crocking is not a shoe. Torqueing is not like planking. Soutaching is not a weird new kind of organic squash. Rattailing is not the furry little friend you have in your basement. And faggoting is not an un-PC term for all of our best friends. Crocking is bleeding of dye; torqueing is twisting of yarn; and soutaching, rattailing, and faggoting are all different kinds of trim. Got it? To source the fabric, we headed downtown to the garment district. We called ahead to ask for directions to the fabric showrooms, but it seemed like we were always getting lost because we were; we're both directionally impaired. We made sales appointments to look at greige goods, another garment industry term for raw fabric that is prepared to take dye. These fabric showrooms were serious establishments, and the salesmen used to look at us like we were crazy in our funkadelic outfits and riding boots. We always liked a lot of the fabrics, but we could only pay a certain price to make our margin. So we spent most of our time reiterating the kind of cotton we wanted. We'd say, "Combed, combed, combed!" and the salesmen would say, "I've got the perfect one for you—carded!" On the drive home, we'd laugh about how the experience reminded us of the *Saturday Night Live* sketch in which people come into a diner asking for all kinds of things, and all Dan Aykroyd will give them is "Cheeseburger, cheeseburger, cheeseburger!"

We loved fabric appointments, because at the end of the day, we love to shop! We looked at hundreds of headers, which is the name for cards with tiny square swatches of fabric attached. To the naked eye, they all looked the same. They were, after all, swatches of white cotton jersey. But when we felt them, we had visceral reactions. It was yes or no, not maybe. They might have been called greige goods, but there was no gray area for us. And that's an important tool for an entrepreneur, to be able to make a decision right or wrong and just roll with it. We could go through a thousand headers like rabbits on speed, because we knew what we liked. And the funny thing is, we always agreed; no matter what pile we were looking through, we always came up with the same likes. We could have done a double-blind test and still picked the same swatches.

In the process, we tried out about twenty or thirty different knits, buying a couple yards of fabric, then test dyeing them, buying and test dyeing, to check for torque and crocking.

On the wall at a showroom called Kronfli Spundale Mills there was an oil portrait of the founder, who we imagined must be named Señor Kronfli, that was like something out of Walt Disney World's Haunted Mansion. We swore the eyes followed us. And because we're the oldest living teenagers in the world, and we thought it was so funny, we wanted to steal it. We have always had a fondness for portraiture. Whenever we were thrifting for clothes, for example, we looked through the paintings and bought the funny ones. Sometimes, we painted over them like the street artist Banksy does, but this was way pre-Banksy. And way worse.

We didn't leave with Señor Kronfli, but we did leave with some of his finest fabric. We had finally found the perfect one-by-one ribbed combed cotton knit in our price range. In reality, the salesman probably got so exasperated that he finally gave it to us for what we could pay. It was the fabric that was going to give us the perfect T-shirt we were dying for.

Fit was the next thing. We went back to the Hanes T-shirt and used ourselves as fit models. It was fit, fit, and fit again. Everything we did was to make your body look as good as it could possibly look. Most male designers don't do that, and they are fitting on perfect models with perfect bodies and no back fat. We tried on our T-shirts with jeans, and made sure that our T-shirt covered that muffin top. Even though we were petite, we didn't have perfect bodies, so we made sure to cover the right part of the arm, and that the waistband wasn't so tight that it cut you in the wrong place. The V-neck had to be sexy but not too sexy. The plunge couldn't be so deep that it made you look trash-tacky.

We were microfitters in a crazy way. We nipped the waists and cut the sleeves, nipped and cut, dozens of times in front of the cheapo mirror we had in our office in Pacoima, before we got the fit the way we liked it. ("Cheapo," by the way, is a word we love. Just because something is more expensive, doesn't mean that it's better.) We drove our sample sewer nuts. Her name was Arshiek, and we had been working with her since our days in the maternity business. Things used to disappear all the time when Arshiek was around. We'd look at each other and say, "What happened to that sample? Where did this go? Where did that go?" One day, we were in the back chatting with Arshiek about the old country. We asked her what she did there, and she said, "Oh, I worked in a meat factory. You know, it was terrible. We had no money and we would steal meat from the factory all the time," she said. "Wherever you worked, you stole." We went back to our office, looked at each other, and said, "Now we know where those samples went. It's part of the culture!" But we didn't mind too much. She did a great job making our samples, and we looked at it as a Juicy perk. God bless America!

Color has always been important to us, and with Juicy, we really did help bring color into T-shirts and the contemporary clothing world. Back then, stores bought T-shirts in black and white and maybe one color. But we wanted a rainbow. Where did our love of color come from? All sorts of places, beginning with the hazy memories of our youth. For Pam, it was hot, sunny summer afternoons in the San Fernando Valley and candy-colored skateboard culture: the neon-colored skate wheels, graphic Robert Williams–designed skate decks, Tony Alva T-shirts, Vans sneakers, and striped tube socks. At age eleven, she started covering her overalls with rainbow embroidery and patches, even patches with meanings she didn't understand. (One patch read "Ski Stoned," another, "Prune Juice Sets You Free.")

For Gela, it was Yves Saint Laurent's Mondrian dresses, Jimi Hendrix's purple passion, David Bowie's glam-rock makeup, and even 1980s club wear. She learned from studying costume design at Carnegie Mellon that colors have meanings and tell stories. And onstage, a color can change an actor's mood and how he carries himself.

As we got older, we expressed our love of color through an endless number of DIY arts and crafts projects. Pam needlepointed colorful squares and geometric patterns, and made abstract acrylic paintings and collage. Gela was a big knitter. When she was pregnant, she used to knit like the woman in the movie *Like Water for Chocolate*. She knitted multicolored coats and dresses, whole outfits. And when Gela had baby Zoe, Pam made her a decoupage crib, with Victorian-era images of babies all over it. It was probably the most toxic thing ever, but it was amazing.

We have always been obsessed with colorful candy, too. From the very beginning, when we used to drive around downtown during the Travis Jeans era, candy was always a part of our day. We'd stop at 7-Eleven or Target and pick up Skittles, Peanut M&M's, Sour Patch Kids, gummy bears, licorice, Blow Pops, whatever. While we were driving around, we soaked up the color in SoCal's multicultural neighborhoods, too, at the Japanese supermarkets in Little Tokyo, the sari stores in Artesia's Little India, and the Latino-owned alternative-medicine botánicas in downtown LA, where we bought the Santeria candle that has been our good-luck charm for twenty years. We streaked our own hair and mixed our own nail polish colors, combining red and black long before Chanel came out with Vamp. We never lost our sense of play. In fact, it became part of our brand culture. If you are an entrepreneur, you have to embrace that childlike quality. Remember when you were in elementary school, and you thought you could do everything? Then by junior high, you knew you couldn't? Well, we skipped that day of school. We have always believed that we could do it, and we could do it our way. You have to believe in yourself first or no one else will.

We wanted everything to be garment-dyed, meaning that instead of using pre-dyed fabric or yarn, the dye is applied after a T-shirt is cut and sewn. We liked the texture and look of it better. (Think back to when you were a kid, making tie-dye garments in a bucket. That kind of process makes the fabric came out soft, textural, and lived-in.) But first, we had to choose the colors we wanted. Since we didn't like the colors offered in the Pantone color book (and it cost something like $3,000 to buy the book!) we went to paint stores, where it was free to look at colors all day—and take home paint chips. We laid out our palette on a piece of cardboard taped with paint chips and snippets of yarn (which were always plentiful, since we were knitters and needlepointers).

The next stop was Almore Dye House, which became our clubhouse for dyeing. It smelled like full-blown chemicals, and there was a guy who worked there named Brody who was totally dye house damaged. He had the reddest eyes we'd ever seen. But we loved him so much, and he eventually came to work for us. We hung out for hours and the owner showed us different techniques. Everyone needs a place like that: a place that believes in you and you can learn from. It goes back to the lesson "Do unto others as you would have them do to you." We were cool with people and they were cool with us. For sure, there are those in our business who were screamers. We weren't like that. We wanted to learn.

We looked through hundreds of cards with swatches of dye in every color you can imagine and then some, trying to match our yarn and paint chips to what was in their inventory. We learned that there were many different blacks—green black, blue black, red black, brown black, and on and on. Same thing with red and white. If they didn't have what we wanted, they made a custom color. Once we decided on the colors, we gave them names, not numbers. We didn't want numbers; that wasn't happy enough. We chose names that had meaning to us, like "Hershey," "petal pink," "summer sun," "blackberry," and "amethyst."

There was a lot of trial and error. When we sent our test fabric to the dye house, the minimum lot was a pound. So we'd throw in little Victorian dresses to dye in colors that we liked. Why not? One of the things we learned is that you have to allow for shrinkage, which happens with the extreme heat involved in the dye process. So if a T-shirt is going to shrink one inch in width and one inch in length, for example, the pattern has to be one inch longer in each place to allow for shrinkage. The people at our dye house taught us a lot of little tricks, too, like to make sure that the colors look good under fluorescent light, which is how you are going to see the garments in stores.

Eventually, we had a V-neck T-shirt in twenty-six Juicy colors, as well as a few coordinating pieces, though those weren't our ticket to the big show. Once we had a sample line, we needed line sheets with all the styles, prices, and colors to take around for sales reps to see if they wanted to represent our line. We doctored it up in a wacky, DIY style, just like we had done with our Sandra Bernhard "Red Hot Mama" maternity campaign. On the cover of the booklet, we used a photo of the famous 1960s-era model Peggy Moffitt wearing LA designer Rudi Gernreich's famous topless bathing suit (we covered the boobs with stars) and random shots of fruit and vegetable stands that we took in downtown LA. We got Old English press-on letters (which became our font of choice for our brand) at the art store to use for type. And inside, we made our own crooked little sketches of all the styles. We Xeroxed the whole thing and had the line sheets spiral-bound at our local copy shop PIPs in Pacoima. We thought it was artsy and amazing. And we know now, it had a vibe. It wasn't corporate, it was just authentically us.

Armed with our sample line and our line sheets, we were ready to find a sales partner, which in the fashion industry is a sales representative with a wholesale showroom to showcase lines. We researched the places that had lines we could relate to and made appointments to bring in our product. The one we really wanted to be in was this fancy showroom called Kirk and Tierney, which represented Free People and Katayone Adeli, which were the happening labels at the time. We headed downtown in Gela's Jeep with our rolling rack packed in the back, set it up in the parking garage, and wheeled it up the elevator into the Cal Mart. (There's someplace like the Cal Mart, which is now named the California Market Center, in every city that has a garment center. It's where the wholesale showrooms are and where retail buyers go to place orders for their stores.) When we went in, the sales reps at Kirk and Tierney were wearing serious fashion 'tude, which was something we couldn't relate to. They were very quiet and reserved and probably dressed in all black. We weren't. But somehow, we managed to convince them to take our line.

The spring 1995 market came around, when buyers came to place their orders at the showroom. And afterward, the reps at Kirk and Tierney wouldn't return our calls for weeks. It turned out that we'd only sold $7,000 worth of product, and they were ready to dump our asses hard and heavy. They told us that our line wasn't right for them (a decision they've since laughed about), but that Lisa Shaller, a sales rep visiting from New York, was just starting her own showroom there and was interested in us.

Lisa, or Shaller, as we call her, was a character, tough but lovable with long, French-tipped nails, a booming laugh, and no fear. She had the craziest New York accent we'd ever heard. One time, she told us a story about how she was going to get a sandwich "felayta." We thought it was a girl's name, and kept saying, "Who's Felayta?" She was saying "a sandwich for later." Although she had just barely opened her showroom, Simply Chic, she had years of Seventh Avenue experience. She started doing sales in New York's garment center at age eighteen, attended the Fashion Institute of Technology, and worked in showrooms for such heavyweight contemporary brands as ABS Allen Schwartz and Laundry. Then, she decided to break out with her own showroom. And she was hungry. She took a trip to LA hoping that she could be the East Coast rep for some cool new lines. She barged into Kirk and Tierney, the hottest showroom at the time, looking for new business, not really knowing that kind of thing wasn't done. She saw in the back corner our colorful pieces on a rolling rack, and our cute, homemade-looking line sheet with pictures of fruits and vegetables on the cover. She asked the sales reps at Kirk and Tierney if she could represent us on the East Coast, and they told her they weren't doing any business with Juicy anyway. She could have it.

When Shaller got back to New York, she called us and told us she wanted to represent Juicy. Gela told her, "If you get it, you can have it," meaning if she understood it, it was hers. Shaller saw something in us that Kirk and Tierney didn't see. She knew from working at previous showrooms that T-shirts weren't really a fashion category yet. But she had a feeling that a new trend was brewing. We sent her a box of samples and she started working the phones, calling all her retailers. She called all her specialty stores in Long Island, NY, and told them, "I have a new T-shirt line to show you." Well, they couldn't have cared less. They said, "We don't need another T-shirt line. Do you know how many Michael Stars T-shirts we sell?" That's one of the most difficult things about the fashion industry. If stores think they have a category covered, they aren't willing to take a risk on a new thing. She got so frustrated that she called the stores again, held her nose to disguise her voice, and said, "Do you carry Juicy?" When they said they only carried Michael Stars, Shaller said, "Michael Stars is for geeks!" and slammed down the phone. That was the Juicy spirit. Phony and prank calls have always been part of our culture. A day doesn't go by without at least one.

So Shaller went back to the drawing board, looked at our box of samples again, and zeroed in on one style, the 103, with cap sleeves and crossover V-neck, the one we had spent months perfecting. That was the shirt that had something to say, she thought, the one that was different from the boxy and baby tees that were already everywhere. She figured out that it might be a lot easier to sell one thing that was great than to beg stores to try a whole new line. She called the retailers again and said, "I know you don't need another line, but how about one perfect T-shirt? I'm asking you to make a five-hundred-dollar commitment to one style in five colors." Well, it worked, and they bought it. Within a year, we had a T-shirt business.

When you are starting a business, you need to build a team around you. Without those people, you're in a vacuum. You could have the most amazing line in your living room, but if you don't find the right person to sell it, it's not going to happen. When you look for a rep, or anyone who is going to help sell your product, find the person who sees your vision, feels the vibe, and wants to take the trip. It should also be someone who's at the right level for what you're trying to do—and someone you can learn from. With Shaller, it felt like we were all in it together. It wasn't like we were the little fish in a big, fancy showroom, being talked down to. Shaller was a partner. She was one of us, digging in the dirt, getting down and dirty. She knew something about a world we didn't know. We were not New York garmentos. Shaller understood trends, how to work with buyers, how to talk to us and to them. She couldn't wait to get her box of clothes, and you never saw her without one of those V-neck T-shirts on. She wore them everywhere, even on vacation, and she looked great in them. She was the perfect rep for a start-up business. She helped us build. If you have people selling your product who are dying for it, you're going to succeed.

Soon after, we got an LA-based rep named Joanne Fiske, someone Shaller recommended. We called her Fiske (we call a lot of people by their last names), and her showroom was the size of a coffin. But we trusted Shaller, so we trusted her. We let Shaller and Fiske do what they did best. We're not micromanagers. But we learned the hard way. One time early in our maternity careers, we went to a sales meeting, and we got so excited, we hung every piece in the entire collection on the grid, which is a huge rolling display on wheels. Well, it got too heavy and fell over. The sales rep said, "Okay, bye bye." We never went to a sales meeting again for a long time. If people are hired to do a job, let them do it—so long as they are doing it well.

We opened all the bigs. Bloomingdale's, Neiman Marcus, Nordstrom, Macy's, Saks, and Barneys became our accounts. Being an LA girl all her life, Pam had never even heard of Bloomingdale's, because the store hadn't opened on the West Coast yet. Shaller said, "What do you mean you don't know Bloomie's? It is a candy store!" Well, those were the magic words. Bloomingdale's played a special role in our story. On a Saturday afternoon, the Fifty-Ninth Street flagship in New York City is like Grand Central Station. You have to duck and dive. It's a critical mass for shopping, and for a fashion brand, it can make or break you. Frank Doroff, the sweet-talking vice-chairman and executive vice president of Bloomingdale's, loves the thrill of the hunt, especially rooting out new trends and labels. The retail landscape was changing. Bridge brands like Dana Buchman and Ellen Tracy were starting to tank, while younger, more casual contemporary brands were starting to explode. Juicy was on the forefront of that explosion and Frank saw an opportunity. So he came out to LA in 1996, and took us to the Polo Lounge at the Beverly Hills Hotel for hot-fudge sundaes. (And every time we saw him at after that, he had hot-fudge sundaes for us, including in the Bloomingdale's executive boardroom.) He said, "I'm going to be your best ally. I'm the only department store that is going to let your brand in my store." He became a mentor and a trusted friend, and helped us take it to the next level.

The first thing he taught us was that we needed to build fixturing for the Fifty-Ninth Street store, meaning we had to build a display to house our T-shirts. We said, "What? We have to pay for that?" It cost about $15,000. What we came up with was pretty bare bones but totally us. We hated seeing T-shirts on hangers because they lost their shape and looked sloppy. We wanted to see folded chunks of color like penny candy at a candy store—you want to buy it all. So we had this crazy sculpture-like thing made with a hanging section on one side and shelves on the other where we could stack chunks of color. It read "Juicy" on the side. At the time, Bloomingdale's was the only store that let you put your brand name on fixturing. We also made a tape for the salespeople to play, because we wanted cool music as part of the shopping experience. Under the music on the tape, we recorded a subliminal message, a woman's voice saying, "Buy Juicy. Buy Juicy. Buy Juicy." We wanted it to sound like HAL in the film *2001: A Space Odyssey*. Now, that's entrepreneurial. Or insane—it's a fine line.

In those days, we didn't know 100 percent what we were doing. And we did use being girls to our advantage. We played dumb. And why not? People used it against us, so we turned it around. We used to play a little game with Frank. He'd say, "It's time for a promotion." And we would say, "Oh my God, it's a free gift with purchase? What do we get today?" Frank said, "No, it's a promotion, meaning the shirts are going on sale, and you have to give us markdown money to cover the discounts we give to customers." We played dumb and told Frank that he needed to give us a department-store dictionary so we could understand what he was talking about with all these terms. In the end, the shirts were selling so well, we ended up not having to pay the markdown money. He used to say we were crazy like foxes. We had bulldozer-like determination, that's for sure. We were going to get our way no matter what. And there is nothing wrong with using naïveté, humor, or just plain being a girl to your advantage, especially in the world of business, where they are going to use all of that to beat you up.

Where Bloomingdale's was our East Coast laboratory, Fred Segal was our West Coast laboratory. Fred Segal was the store that every buyer in the country visited to see what was hot and happening. John Eshaya was the incredible buyer and creative director there at the time, and he helped define Southern California style by discovering and guiding brands like ours. He got Juicy from day one, and understood that the idea of the brand was very California, very evocative of the famous 1977 photo of Farrah Fawcett on a skateboard in that red sweatshirt, jeans, and Nikes. John bought our first T-shirt in eight colors, stacked them up on a table in the pit, and told every girl she had to wear them. That's the kind of power he had in those days: He could tell people what to wear. And this was before the era of big celebrity stylists, so all of the Hollywood "It" girls shopped at Fred Segal, where they followed John's advice and loaded up on the T-shirts. Costume designers shopped there, too. That's how our T-shirts started to show up on the cast of *Friends*.

We were starting to have big orders—$300,000 big. And we should have been raking in the money. But we were just breaking even. It's called turning dollars. At the time, our accounting firm was Moss Adams, which was like the Kirk and Tierney of the accounting world. Every few months, the guys from Moss Adams used to come out to our crappy warehouse in Pacoima wearing their slick suits and go over our books. They told us we weren't making money, something we knew very well. But they never dug deep enough to find out why. They breezed in and out, treating us like dumb girls, and never giving us the time of day, even though it was their job to give us a financial road map. We expected them to tell us if we were spending too much on sampling or office expenses. Finally, we hit a wall. We made them sit down and tell us why, if our orders were so big, weren't we making any money? And they said, "Well, isn't it obvious? You're not costing right." "Are you kidding?" we said. "You've been our accountants this whole time and you're just now telling us we're not costing right? We look to you to advise us. How could that be?" Well, it was because they never took us seriously. We were just Pam and Gela, two wacky girls from the Valley.

What we were doing wrong was not adding in all the actual costs of making our garments, and building in enough of a markup to make a profit. We were doing our cost sheets in a very rudimentary way, with line items for cutting, sewing, dyeing, and shipping. Then we added in an extra dollar for a markup—we called it the WTF dollar. But that wasn't enough for us to make a profit. It turned out, we also weren't adding in all the complexities of selling to department stores or catalogs, which involves a ton of little fees. We were looking for a financial partner to teach us what we didn't understand, but Moss Adams was too big to give us the attention we needed. We found another accounting firm, one better suited to the needs of a small company. Jay Mangel was kind of like the Lisa Shaller of accountants. His firm wasn't as prestigious as Moss Adams, not as Ivy League, but he was right for Juicy, and right nearby in Sherman Oaks.

You can find the wrong rep, who sells $7,000, or you can find the right rep, who grows your business. You can hire the wrong accountant who gives you zero advice on what's going down, or you can find the right one who is digging deep and telling you what you need to tweak and change. The bottom line is this: You don't have to go to business school to have a successful business. But you do have to find a team of people at the right level to help you. It took us a while, but at last, we had the first few members of our team in place. Stores were reordering the shirts as fast as they could get them. And that was okay, because we believe in the KFC theory—do one thing, and do it well. The product was great and people wanted it. We had sales of $1 million by the end of 1995, and $5 million by the end of 1996.

Our reps and buyers were calling every day, asking, "So, what's the next big T-shirt?" We'd say, "Ummm, it's in the safe, and when we remember the combination, we'll open it up and let you know." We were feeling the pressure. We couldn't rest on our laurels. People were starting to trust our name and they wanted more.

The KFC Theory Is Not Just for Chicken: Do One Thing and Do It Well

What's the one thing you want and can't find the perfect iteration of? Go out there and create it.

Figure out your brand DNA. Ours was fit, fabric, and color. What is going to be your mantra, the three- to four-word guiding principle for every choice you make and thing you say about your product?

Try to use the resources in your backyard. That way, your business will be more nimble.

When it comes to production, find a person or place that believes in you, and that you can learn from. Don't go somewhere so big that you'll get lost in the shuffle and not be able to communicate with the people doing the work for you. They are your lifeline.

You don't have to go to business school to have a successful business, but you do need the right team around you. Find an accountant, a sales rep, and a lawyer, and cultivate a group of retail partners.

Don't worry about hiring the best. Find the person who is hungry, sees your vision, feels the vibe, and wants to take the trip. That's the person who treats you like a partner.

Once you hire someone to do a job, let them do it—as long as they are doing it well. No one likes a boss looking over their shoulder.

There is nothing wrong with using naïveté, humor, or just plain being a girl to your advantage, especially in the world of business, where people are going to use all of that to beat you up.

Glossary of Business Terms

Costing: Tallying up the cost of everything you're paying for that goes into making a product, including the WTF dollar. You have to mark up the price of your product above that to make money.

Defect: Something damaged, like a velour jacket that's a J-pull zipper charm away from being Juicy.

Factor: A big expensive meanie who makes you have an adding machine with a tape, but who will screen all the boutiques you're selling to and make sure they are credit-worthy. A factor assumes responsibility for being paid by the stores and advances you cash so you can manufacture and ship. (They take a percentage for taking the risk.) You have to love factors because they are how small businesses get off the ground. They are loan sharks, and you have to kiss the ring.

Fulfillment house: Not the place where all your dreams come true, but the place where all the stuff gets shipped out to go to the stores—which makes everyone else's dreams come true.

Line sheet: The presentation on paper of your collection, including each style with prices, colors, and delivery dates. Can also be an art project, like it was for us in the beginning! Used by your sales rep to sell the collection.

Manufacturing vs. Production: Both are terms for the process of converting materials into a product on a large scale. The difference is in the details. If you own the resources and materials, then you are producing; if you are getting them from outside sources, you're manufacturing.

Margin: Not a place to doodle, but rather the money you get to keep after you sell a product. Gross margin is before all the costs are factored in and net margin is after all the costs are factored in.

Markdown money: A dirty word you never want to admit you know. If your product doesn't sell at full price and has to be marked down, stores want you to absorb some of the costs by giving them money back. It's a perpetual negotiation.

Marketing: Has nothing to do with going to Whole Foods. It's how you tell the world what you stand for, and reach out and grab your customer by shouting from the rooftops, "Get your Juicy T-shirts right here!"

Returns: What you never want to take. It's when stores try to give you things back that don't sell, arrive late, or are damaged. How do you keep from getting them? Make kick-ass product.

Sample line: Sample pieces that your sales team goes to market with. Can also be sent out to press to photograph or celebrities to wear.

Shrinkage: Loss of inventory due to theft, paperwork errors, and the like. It's a fact of life when you're doing business. Or, in the case of T-shirts, how much fabric shrinks after being garment-dyed.

SKU: Has nothing to do with your hat being on sideways. SKU is the acronym for "stock-keeping unit" that's the unique identifier for each product. It includes attributes such as manufacturer, material, size, and color.

Sourcing: Has nothing to do with the Source restaurant on Sunset Boulevard that's famously featured in *Annie Hall.* It's finding what you need to make your product, including materials, factories, and services, at the right price.

Chapter 5

What's in a Name?

In the late 1990s, fashion was on the cusp of a major change. Women were starting to dress down and they liked it. The idea of business casual was sweeping the nation, thanks to the dot-com bubble, and office attire was loosening up. Women were buying T-shirts by the armload in every color and wearing them under their business suits as a way to have fun with fashion. It created an opportunity for a brand like ours, but also a challenge.

The more T-shirts became hot-selling items, the more players jumped into the game. We have always kept our eyes on what's happening in the market, scoping out Fred Segal, Barneys, Maxfield, and other stores to see what is new and what is selling, which is something every entrepreneur should do. What we noticed was that there were a lot more T-shirts selling next to ours. It seemed like a new brand was launching every day, and we felt them at our heels. We could have freaked out, but we didn't. Competition can be healthy. It meant we were on to something, and it drove us to be better. But it was time to sound the rebel yell. We have always said, "No need to look around and no need to look back. Look forward." We knew we were at a crossroads and needed to figure out a way to elevate our product and stand out from the pack. It was time to start tweaking the business to grow, beginning with our name.

When we started Juicy in 1995, we were just coming out of a recession. It was a time when people still wanted to pay a little less—a nickel off a yard of fabric here, a dime off the cost of sewing there. As the decade went on, the economy not only improved, it boomed. All of a sudden, everyone wanted a luxury T-shirt (and bag and shoes). They actually wanted to pay more! We thought, What are we going to do with that? How are we going to compete? If our product wasn't expensive or didn't seem expensive, it wasn't going to work in the new fashion order.

We started thinking about the most fundamental building block of our business: the name. We needed a name that made our shirts sound not only colorful and fun, but like the most luxe T-shirts out there. So we convened for another one of our brainstorming sessions, and came up with every word we could think of that could help elevate our product to the nth degree. "Juicy the Collection" didn't have the right ring to it, and neither did "House of Juicy." But "couture," as in the old world, high-end French tradition of hand-sewn, made-to-measure clothes—now, that was *super* luxe. And like everything we did, there was a sense of irony to it, because what could be more ironic than a pairing of the highest of the high with the lowest of the low, a casual T-shirt line called Juicy Couture?

Since then, the word "couture" has become part of pop culture. It's been taken by nearly every other company on the planet. There are couture bathroom tiles and kitchen faucets. POM Wonderful pomegranate juice had a "Juice Couture" ad campaign. There are the Disney Couture and Wildfox Couture clothing lines. "Couture" is a massive word in the name game. But it was a big decision for Juicy to become Juicy Couture, and one we thought about long and hard. We had to trademark and pay for the name, throw out thousands of labels and hangtags and manufacture new ones. Not everyone understood it. Our sales rep Lisa Shaller said, "What is that, 'Juicy Cooter?' No one will be able to pronounce it!" But we thought Juicy Couture was brilliant, as we think everything we do is brilliant until we find out it isn't. That's the way you have to look at things when you're an entrepreneur. Full steam ahead!

Next, we turned our attention to the product. People were hot on our trail, so we had to keep spinning out new designs to stay ahead of them. We added different fabrications, styles, and colors, until we had more than T-shirts: We had a full line of casual knit tops in baby rib cotton, waffle-weave cotton, and more. When we started, our T-shirts cost between $21 and $30. We then raised our prices to between $30 and $60. We also changed our sizing from 1, 2, 3, to XS, S, M, L, which gave our customer a more exacting fit and increased our sales, because stores had to order more to have a full size range. Each season, we showed twenty-six colors, and buyers chose black, white, and two colors. But that started changing. We told them they had to buy five colors because we wanted to see chunks of color on the shelves in the store. And that helped our sales, too.

We were trying to bust out, so we made every manifestation of T-shirt we could think of— three-quarter sleeve, baseball, henley, half-cap sleeve, tank, 1970s tank, Jackie O boatneck, and on and on. We used to joke about all the styles, saying, "cap, half-cap, cap-cap" sounded like a Starbucks order. One of our biggest successes was a tank top twinset, a three-quarter-sleeve cardigan in T-shirt fabric that you wore over a matching tank top. Barneys New York even put them in their windows, and styled them with ball skirts that we made out of sari fabric from Artesia. (The casual top-and-ball-skirt look was a big trend at the time, after Sharon Stone wore a Gap turtleneck and Valentino ball skirt to the 1996 Academy Awards.)

We did a three-quarter-sleeve shrug and a cap-sleeve shrug. We couldn't sell enough of them. Then one day, they died. We were washing our cars with them. Everywhere we went, we found new ideas. As a designer and an entrepreneur, you always have to keep your eyes and ears open. It wasn't a chore for us, because this was the kind of research we wanted to do, whether it was soaking in the art and architecture at the Museum of Contemporary Art in downtown LA, scouring fashion history books, or sifting through vintage pieces at thrift stores. Gela shopped the vintage stalls on Portobello Road in London and came back with a 1970s-era Coca-Cola baseball tee with red sleeves that inspired us. And one night, when she was at a restaurant in LA, she noticed the waitress was wearing a corset-style T-shirt she had poked holes in and laced up the back. We ended up making a T-shirt like that.

We could find ideas anywhere, from common objects like the ICEE maker at our local convenience store, to cigarette packages, to Barbara Kruger art installations. We've always been obsessed with logos and packaging, we don't care if it's from the 99¢ only store or Hermès. We'd sit around brainstorming, flipping through magazines, and coming up with funny twists on things in pop culture. We started making funny logo tees with sayings like "Dump Him," "ICEE Juicy," and "Glamour Puss." There was "Dude, Where's My Couture?" (which came from the Ashton Kutcher film *Dude, Where's My Car?*), "Choose Juicy" (after Katharine Hamnett's "Choose Life" slogan tees from the 1980s), "I Want Candy" (after the Bow Wow Wow song), "Smells Like Couture" (after the Nirvana song "Smells Like Teen Spirit"), "McQueen of the Fucking Universe" (a reference to the designer Alexander McQueen; we sent him one of the T-shirts and he loved it), and other things we just thought were silly, like "Don't Be a Bitch" (because we don't like mean-girl culture, and there are a lot of bitches in the fashion arena).

We came up with some clever ideas for packaging the shirts, too. On one of our daily candy runs to Pick 'n Save next to our office, we noticed all of these clear vinyl backpacks that were piped in colors. "Do you have more of those?" we asked. "We want hundreds." We sewed our own Juicy Couture labels inside and stuffed each bag with tissue paper, candy, and a T-shirt. Everyone loved them. We even got press on those bags: a mention in *Glamour* magazine. Those clear backpacks still have resonance. They have a rave-kid vibe.

We were really starting to have fun thinking about all sorts of products we could make, not just T-shirts. Everything we saw in the world, we wanted to flip and turn into something Juicy. It was a business, but it was also our outlet for pop art–like expression. After all, just like Peter Morton with the Hard Rock Café, we wanted to create a whole Juicy empire. One of our favorite logo tees was a riff on Hermès's famous Paris address on Rue de Faubourg. Our shirt read "Rue de Branford, Pacoima." We made notepads, mints, and matches, even a cashmere sweater, all in Hermès orange with the address "Rue de Branford, Pacoima." Well, Hermès wasn't so amused. Their legal team sent us a letter to cease and desist. We thought the letter was so funny, we framed it and put it on the wall in our office, but not before we called the Hermès lawyers and asked them if they could resend it on official orange Hermès stationery with brown ink! (Again, they were not amused.) This was our first run-in with any kind of legal issue, and we weren't daunted—we were excited! It made us feel like we were in the big leagues. We were on their radar.

Humor is part of who we are, so, of course, it became part of the culture of our brand. Another part of our culture was that our clothes were, as we put it, "Made in the Glamorous U.S.A." We had those words printed proudly on our labels from day one. It was important to us that our shirts be made in the United States. If we were going to make it, we wanted our community to make it. We didn't want to go offshore; we wanted to create jobs for people here and keep it in our backyard. That value came from our Republican fathers, and from the fact that we were too scared to manufacture so far away from home that we couldn't keep an eye on things. That's why we used local contractors in the beginning. We wanted to see it and touch it, make sure it was right and be able to make changes. You have to be on top of your product. When you lose that connection, and you can't see what you're making on a day-to-day, week-to-week basis, it gets away from you.

We kept everything close. We used the resources in our own backyard, including a knitwear contractor we found through our old maternity business buddy Bruce. We were still in the same office park in Pacoima where we had worked in the Travis Jeans days, self-contained in Unit G with a warehouse in the back. And because everyone was nearby, it made the production and shipping aspects of our business run that much more smoothly.

Our knitwear factory was right across the street. The factory owner, Angela Torti, schooled us in everything to do with knits. She was this big Italian grandmother type with a lovingly loud voice that could cut glass. She held her grandbaby in her arms up and walked up and down the sewing lines, shouting orders. She knew what was going to work and not work from a practical sewing perspective and she guided us. One time, after she finished sewing up a shirt, she told us that the sleeves were so tight you wouldn't be able to get your arms in after the shirt was dyed. So we had to start all over again with that style. She taught us that if we were making a tank top, it needed to have an invisible ribbon of elastic sewn into the neckline to keep it from stretching out. She taught us that if you put a T-shirt on and heard tiny "ripping" noises, that meant the thread was not sewn with the proper tension. Knowing all these little tricks of the trade just made our shirts better and better.

At first, it was just the two of us going everywhere together—to the knitwear factory, the dye house, and back to the office for fittings and to work on accounts receivable. But that was very time-ineffective. So we started to build our Juicy team in an organic way. In the beginning, you don't have to place a "Help Wanted" ad or hire a fancy headhunting firm to build a team. We built our staff like a family, by networking with people we knew and through word of mouth. We hired people because we had a gut feeling for them—just like we did about each other when we first became partners and friends. If somebody was a hard worker, had a passion, and showed initiative, we saw something in them, too.

We never really had titles, because we think titles are limiting. Plus, everyone wears more than one hat in a small business. And in an entrepreneurial environment, we've found that people can find their own way. Besides, we wanted a collaborative experience, where people could share their ideas on everything from how to organize the warehouse to design. Our door was always open. At our company, there was no glass ceiling. You could grow and create a position for yourself. We didn't know we were setting people up to succeed, but that was natural.

Our first employee was Elva Gonzalez, who was a cousin of Gela's babysitter. We needed someone to clean our office, and Elva was looking for work. She started cleaning for us once a week, and one day, after noticing how many boxes we were packing and labeling ourselves to ship out, she said, "I can do that for you." She was a self-motivated soul who wanted to do more. And more. She started packing boxes, then suggested a better way to organize our racks of clothing. As we became bigger, Elva arranged pickups from the contractors and drop-offs at dye houses, sort shirts for damages, fill purchase orders, print shipping labels, and have boxes ready for pickup by UPS. She learned how to ship to a department store and how to take inventory (which we did with an abacus but somehow it worked). She learned as we learned. One day, she was mopping the floor, and the next day she was hiring her own team of people to pick and pack shirts, and running our warehouse up until we had a $40 million business. That's America.

Instead of outsourcing to a fulfillment house, we shipped out of the back of our offices, which saved us a ton of money. Fulfillment houses are supposed to make logistics easier, but they can be money suckers. At the time, for us, it didn't work. They charged a flat fee for each shirt, say $1.50, which included the labor to pick it up from the contractor, count it, press it, fold it, tag it, put it in a bag, box it, and ship it. The problem was, some of the shirts "fell off the truck" between the dye house and the fulfillment house, and then some more shirts were dropped because they didn't make the cut. We lost way too much of our merchandise. So we brought it back in-house, and we didn't lose a single shirt. If it was flawed, Elva saw to it that the shirt was repaired or redyed and then sent out. It was very cost-effective, and we had no waste.

Because everything was manufactured close by in the beginning, the business was nimble and we could react to trends and turn around reorders in as little as three weeks. (When you manufacture overseas, it takes eight to ten weeks to turn around a reorder, if it's even possible.) If a store wanted to reorder three hundred black Juicy Couture T-shirts, for example, someone ran across the street to Angela Torti's factory, put the shirts in bags, and took them to the dye house. Whoever was around did it, including us. When you are in a small business, it's kind of a free-for-all, and you have to find people who are ready and willing to jump in. You don't want to hire anyone who is uptight or entitled, who would say, "I wasn't hired to do this!" Those kinds of people don't belong at a start-up. We expected our employees to do anything, because we did . . . to a point.

One time, Pam was in the warehouse, reaching for a shirt on the bottom shelf, and she came face-to-face with a rat noshing on a baguette. He had a full-on condo back there. We were screaming like babies, but Elva knew how to handle it. She called her uncle and he came and took care of the little guy. That's how we did things on all levels. Everyone had a friend or a family member who could pitch in, which was good, because we may have been fearless entrepreneurs, but our fearlessness stopped with rodentia.

Another member of our Juicy team who was critical to our success was Vicki Goldshtein, who was with us thirteen years. We needed someone to input all the store orders into the computer. We heard about Vicki from our West Coast sales rep, Joanne Fiske, who met her when she was an intern at the Cal Mart. Vicki was a kick-ass Russian girl who was young and hungry. Her parents, Alex and Anna Goldshtein, had an embroidery factory called A&A Embroidery, which we ended up turning to a lot, including for the bias trim for our T-shirts. We thought we would give Vicki a try, so we had her come in and enter some invoices. When her fingers hit the keys, smoke started to come off that computer. She could type faster than we had ever seen! We said, "Okay, you've got this under control, we're going to lunch!" (By lunch, we meant Taco Bell, which was one of our standbys. We've never been the ladies-who-lunch types; we eat on the fly. There was too much to do during the day, and besides, there wasn't really anywhere to go in Pacoima anyway.)

Vicki's role was not designed. She did what needed to get done. Because she was entering all the purchase orders and keeping track of our sales, she was in constant contact with retail accounts. She took note of what was selling well, and what colors were reordered. As we got bigger, Vicki sat in sales meetings, too, and heard feedback that way. She morphed into our merchandiser, helping us fine-tune the assortment in the line (the colors and bodies, for example) to make sure every store had what they needed to sell and grow.

Unlike at a lot of other fashion companies, you didn't have to dress to impress us. In our office, pajama dressing was encouraged. We once interviewed a candidate to do bookkeeping—Babs was her name—who showed up in a silk blouse, tight pencil skirt, and heels. She got the job, but we told her to come to work in anything but that, even if it was her pajamas. The point is, we wanted our work environment to be loose and for people to be comfortable. We encouraged our employees to live the California casual lifestyle because that's what our brand was about. People were happy. They brought their dogs to work. We did, too. Because, the truth is, you can't be productive and creative in an office environment that's ruled by fear. We care about our employees, we care about each other, and we care about our customers. We believe if a product is made with love, it's made with an authentic, real, caring way. And the customer can feel that.

In the beginning, we had a revolving cast of funny receptionists, all of whom were from a temp agency. Juicy wasn't that well known then, and people used to call and ask what kinds of juices we were selling. We had a receptionist we didn't realize was deaf in one ear until we started getting unintelligible handwritten messages like "Osada called." Gela called the number back and it was her father! We had another receptionist with a Castilian accent who used to answer the phone, "Hello, Juthy." A third receptionist was so OCD, she taped shut the candy jar full of "Rue de Branford" notepads we had on her desk for guests, because she didn't want anyone taking them. These people were all part of our crazy family.

Family is everything. We wanted that experience at work and at home. In 1997, Gela met and fell in love with her future husband, John Taylor from Duran Duran. It was a match made in fashion heaven. On their first date, they went to a Sex Pistols concert. On their second date, John brought Gela a stack of French and Italian *Vogue* magazines. He loved clothes as much as she did. And although she didn't know much about music, Gela could relate to the sense of family John had with his bandmates, and the way they believed in themselves. They were changing with the musical times, just as Juicy Couture was changing with the fashion times. In March 1999, Gela and John married in a small ceremony in Las Vegas, and got to work blending their two families—Atlanta from John's previous marriage, and Travis and Zoe from Gela's.

Pam and her husband, Jef, were trying to start their own family. Sadly, Pam had a late-term miscarriage, which was heart-wrenching. That's where partners and friends came in. Pam leaned on Gela, who stepped in and picked up the slack. But the experience made Pam more determined than ever to get pregnant again. And getting back to work helped her through the pain and sadness.

Our little company was growing, but we were still desperately trying to come up with the next big thing—something, anything but a shirt. In business, and in life, you've got to know how to bob and weave.

Up until then, we had only been selling Juicy Couture in the United States. We figured one way to grow our business was to get an international distributor to sell our shirts in Asia. In 1999, John signed a contract with the Japanese record label Avex Trax, and planned to travel there to record a solo album. Gela decided she would use the opportunity to get a contract of her own with a Japanese distributor—and have a short honeymoon in Kyoto.

Japan was ground zero for what was hot and happening in fashion, and the Japanese were in love with American culture and American brands. There was a lot of cross-cultural exchange going on already. Our friend Sofia Coppola, who appeared in Jef's film *Inside Monkey Zetterland*, had launched a line called Milk Fed in 1994, which was so successful in Japan, that she eventually sold it to her Japanese distributors. Sonic Youth's Kim Gordon and stylist Daisy von Furth did the same thing with their line X-Girl, which really defined how cool girls like Chloë Sevigny, Ione Skye, and Coppola dressed in the early 1990s. So we thought there could be opportunity for Juicy there.

We were doing $20 million in sales at the time, which was nothing to sneeze at. But it was still basically just a shirt business. Getting a distributor in Japan wasn't pie in the sky, but it wasn't too far from it. Still, we have always believed in thinking big. So Joanne Fiske set up a meeting for Gela with the Japanese distributor Sanei International in Tokyo. When she got there, she put on her fiercest outfit and headed to the top floor of the Sanei office building. Gela went by herself—*by herself*—into a boardroom full of men in suits and clouds of thick cigarette smoke. The only other woman in there was pouring tea. Drawing on all her entrepreneurial fearlessness, and a little bit of her acting training, too, she proceeded to tell the good fellows at Sanei why they should sign a deal to distribute Juicy Couture throughout Japan. She went on and on about the T-shirts, and how they were selling at Fred Segal and Neiman Marcus. But they didn't care. What they were interested in was denim. And denim is what we gave them.

Even before the Japan trip, we had been working on developing a line of Juicy Jeans. We thought that denim could be the next big category to grow our business, and it was a natural. Number one, we had done jeans before with Travis. Number two, Earl Jean had launched in 1996 with a sexy, low-slung style that made a huge splash not only in LA but internationally, so we had a feeling that jeans were the next big category on the horizon. And number three, jeans and T-shirts—come on! They go together like chips and salsa. With denim, our goal was the same as with our T-shirts: to create jeans that made your body look insane. We were obsessed with cheating seams forward to make the legs look thinner. And we wanted a straight, squared-off waistband, not a curved one, which looked too Gloria Vanderbilt for us.

By then, we had an in-house patternmaker named Jan Matthey to help us. To develop the perfect fit, we went through the same process as the T-shirts. We tweaked and tweaked and tweaked and tweaked and tweaked. She went along with our microfitting insanity. And it wasn't easy. We used to joke about how we were caught in the Bermuda Triangle of denim, because we were trying to create a pair of jeans in dark denim that was soft, which was kind of an oxymoron. If you wash dark denim over and over again to try to get it soft, it fades. The shrinkage was hard to control, too. We kept sending the jeans to the wash house over and over and somehow, they always came back bigger than when they left. We went crazy!

By the time we perfected the first collection of Juicy Jeans, we had a full range of styles, including an ultra-low-rise straight leg, a boot cut, and super-bell-bottoms. We also had a lot of washes, ten- and fourteen-ounce weights, and stretch and nonstretch fabric. On the inside of the waistband, we had different logoed labels, depending on the style—a heart, a flag, or the slogan "Have a Juicy Day." And on the outside of the waistband, we put a "J" for Juicy. We were always thinking about details and branding.

Sanei agreed to give the T-shirt business to us if we gave the denim to them. We signed a three-year, $3 million deal guaranteeing us $1 million the first year. We surpassed that. And it gave us the ability to grow Juicy Couture even more. It meant more hires, more fabric, and more product extensions. The day our jeans hit the shelves in Japan, we broke a store record. We sold $82,000 worth of jeans in a single day. We were officially big in Japan.

We got a lot out of that first experience selling internationally. It was the first time we realized that Juicy Couture had the potential to be a global brand. We also learned something about how to position ourselves with PR and marketing. The Japanese thought "Made in America" was cool, but they thought "Made in LA" was cooler. We were an LA brand and we learned the power of that. LA had an X factor. And our hook was going to be bringing LA style to the world. One of Sanei's strategies was to have Gela meet the press before the launch. She spent three days doing interviews for every magazine in the country. Then, when Juicy Jeans launched in the stores, women already knew about it. There were lines around the block of people waiting for the stores to open! We did the same thing later on when we opened in London. We went in before our collection hit the stores and did a lot of advance press.

The trip was a full-on success. John got a record, Gela got a honeymoon, and we got a distribution deal. Three years later, when Gela returned to Japan to negotiate the second one, she asked for $10 million. And she got it.

But first, it was time to party. We wanted to launch Juicy Jeans in America, and we wanted to do it right. It was time to hire a publicist. We lived in a bubble in LA. We'd never been to New York Fashion Week or to a New York fashion party. We didn't have a clue about that world. So we asked a friend who was tapped into both the LA and New York fashion scenes to suggest a few public relations firms. We ended up hiring Harrison & Shriftman. We worked with cofounder Lara Shriftman, who was known for producing great events for the likes of Mercedes-Benz, Jimmy Choo, and *InStyle* magazine, and later wrote several books about party planning.

We've always felt, no matter what we do, people need to have fun. We weren't those uptight, serious, we're-going-to-have-a-presentation-at-our-showroom-and-introduce-our-jeans type of designers. We didn't even want to have a fashion show at the event. We just wanted to have a blowout, a fun, crazy party with entertainment. Because if we didn't want to go, who the hell was going to want to?

Well, we didn't know what we were in store for. We chose a date, November 10, 1999, and came up with an idea for the invitation, which was an actual jeans pocket with all the party details embroidered on it in orange thread. (Creative invitations have always been a specialty of ours, and these were embroidered at Vicki's parents' factory.) Lara chose the venue, Joe's Pub, which was a hot music club on Lafayette Street, and drafted a guest list of editors, store buyers, socialites, and celebrities. She also sent out jeans to a lot of the guests ahead of time so they would wear them to the event and get photographed for the press coverage that came out in *Interview* magazine, *New York* magazine, and *Women's Wear Daily*. It was a genius strategy, and one that we continued to use for years.

For the entertainment, Gela worked her magic. John wasn't together with Duran Duran at the time. But, after Gela and John ran into Simon Le Bon one afternoon at Barneys New York in Beverly Hills, Gela persuaded them to reunite and play a set for the event. Well, everyone had to come and check that out, and they wanted to bring their boyfriends and husbands, too. Lara told us that nobody turned down the invitation. It was shaping up to be an amazing night.

By then, we were dressing alike a lot of the time. Even if we didn't call each other, or talk about what we were going to wear beforehand, we showed up in the same outfit. So it became a funny thing that we did. And it was also a great branding tool—the two-best-friends branding tool. People always recognized us, even if they couldn't always tell us apart. That night, we wore black ball skirts and black football jerseys decorated with rhinestones that read "Juicy

00." When we got to Joe's Pub, we couldn't believe there was a red carpet. A red carpet for a jeans launch? It seemed weird to us, but we trusted Lara. And people kept pouring in all night.

Once the party was really rolling, we got onstage and introduced John, who started with a solo set. Then, joined by Simon, they ripped into the Power Station hit "Some Like It Hot" and the Duran Duran hit "Rio," which became a massive singalong. People didn't want to leave! One editor got so tipsy, she threw her bra onstage! There must have been 250 guests when the FDNY showed up to say the venue was at capacity and they were going to shut us down if anyone else came in.

Looking back now, that Juicy Jeans party broke the mold. Today, all fashion parties are like ours was then. You expect a red carpet and a musical guest. But things were more serious in the late 1990s, when Ralph Lauren, Donna Karan, and Calvin Klein were still the biggest names in town. We're not sure that people knew what to make of us, two best friends from LA who dressed alike and loved to have fun. But that's who we were. And we weren't done yet—far from it.

Competition Can Be Healthy

Bring it on! It means you're on to something. And it drives you to be better. But it also means it's time to sound the rebel yell and up your game.

Keep your eye on the market and how your product is positioned, and read trends. What's new and what's selling around your product?

How can you stand out from the pack?

Could you be doing more by simply adding more sizes, colors, or features?

How can you elevate your product and/or packaging?

Are there other markets you should look at, or channels of distribution? Don't be afraid of thinking big, as in global, when it comes to expansion.

What characteristic does your brand have that your competition doesn't? For us, it was the cool factor of LA. Use that as a point of differentiation.

Look for new inspiration everywhere you go—at art museums, on the street, even at your local convenience store. Be open.

Think about your personal brand, too. For us, dressing alike started off as a joke but ended up being a powerful branding tool.

Build Your Staff Like a Family

Don't worry about going to a fancy headhunter at first.

Network with friends and family and use word of mouth to find candidates.

Build a team based on your gut feeling about people. They should be hardworking and show passion and initiative.

No titles; in a small business, everyone wears more than one hat. People should not be so uptight that they won't pitch in and help where they're needed.

Set people up to succeed.

Let them find their own way and create a role that's based on their strengths.

Keep them challenged by letting them try new things and take on new responsibilities.

Bash the idea of a glass ceiling. At Juicy, our first employee was a babysitter/housekeeper who offered to help us pack boxes and ended up running our warehouse.

Reward creativity and success not just with words but with actions.

Encourage employees to live the lifestyle of your brand. For us, that meant wear sweatpants to work!

Keep your door open (for feedback, open communication, and ideas).

Be upbeat and cultivate a culture of fun. People can't be productive and creative in an office environment ruled by fear.

Chapter 6
Building the Glitter Factory

Juicy was already the cool brand on every fashion girl's list, and our worth was growing steadily, from $24 million to $26 million to $30 million. But with growth, you always have to keep reinventing. And Juicy Jeans didn't rock the world. Everything isn't a hit, which is an important thing to remember when you have a business. The jeans certainly didn't take off like some of the other brands coming out of Southern California at the time, such as Earl Jean, Frankie B, and J Brand, which created a whole new premium denim category in the apparel market. We hadn't yet hit on the thing that would be a game changer for Juicy Couture and for the way women dressed the world over. But we were about to.

By now, you know that we didn't have a traditional office environment, or even traditional titles, which we find limiting. If one of us had to step away for a few months, the other stepped in to pick up the slack. That's one of the perks of being your own boss and having a friend as a business partner. In 1999, Pam got the best Christmas present ever. She found out she was pregnant again and she was over the moon. But, because the pregnancy was high risk, she had to be on bed rest from March all the way through July. That's when she developed her exceptional computer skills and became obsessed with all things tech including online shopping, which was to become the way of the future. Online trading, eBay, you name it. It opened up another world. She could have been a stockbroker, she learned so much. But she still missed the day-to-day office routine and called in at least ten times a day. "What's going on?" Pam said. "The same thing that was going on when you called thirty minutes ago," Gela answered. We organized bedside design sessions at Pam's house in Laurel Canyon, and brought her swatches and samples. She was still involved to say the least, which was important, because in a small business collaboration is what makes you grow.

The thing that's great about a small, entrepreneurial work environment is that the people working with you become like a family. We had assembled the foundation of our Juicy team—our sales reps, Lisa Shaller in New York and Joanne Fiske in LA; our jack-of-all-trades, Vicki Goldshtein; queen of our warehouse, Elva Gonzalez; our patternmaker, Jan Matthey; and our publicist, Lara Shriftman. It was a fun, crazy place. In the office, our favorite toy was the intercom system. We sang over the loudspeaker, we talked over the loudspeaker, we told jokes and did funny voices. Everyone felt the excitement of the brand momentum. When you walked into Juicy Couture, you had to pass by our office. The door was never closed, and we listened to our employees. As an entrepreneur, you have to be open to suggestions. It took all of us to take the brand to the next level. Everyone brought something to the party that was part of who we were and what we became. When companies get bigger, everybody just wants to stay in their lane and not make waves. But we were never scared of big waves, and Laird Hamilton had nothing on us.

We wanted to hear what everyone was feeling about the fit, feel, and overall vibe of the collection because the women who worked with us were the women we wanted to dress. We all tried everything on—that was our culture. And we knew we had a hit when everyone in the office became obsessed with a product, from the funkiest girl to the most conservative girl. We weren't divas or megalomaniacs. Ideas got thrown into the pot, and sometimes they stuck. We wanted the Warhol Factory, or maybe we should call it the Glitter Factory—an amazing, creative place where not only could our company grow, but our employees could thrive, too.

We were selling tops and jeans. But Juicy Couture needed more, more, more, if it was going to become a full-fledged lifestyle brand. Shaller kept telling us to design knit pants to go with the tops, fill out the line, and grow the business, because knit pants would be a natural progression from our origins in the knit top business. It was the right instinct, because even when you introduce new products, you still have to be true to that first thing that's you. For Ralph Lauren, it's the polo shirt. For us, it was the T-shirt. But knit pants? They didn't seem like something we would wear . . . more like something our grannies would wear. We couldn't get past the idea that they would be clingy and unflattering, and we were superconcerned about . . . well, let's just say it rhymes with "mammal show."

But the idea of pants that matched the Juicy colors of our shirts was something that resonated with us. We had long conversations about how we wanted to design a modern-day uniform of coordinating pieces that women could throw on to create a monochromatic look and instantly feel put together. (One of the alternate names for our company, if you remember, was Uniform.) We wanted a no-brainer, Garanimals wardrobe experience—a *chic* Garanimals wardrobe experience. If you don't know, Garanimals is a line of children's clothing launched in 1972 on the idea of easy-to-match separates. Each item features an anthropomorphic character on the hangtag, so children can easily dress themselves by choosing matching items with matching hangtags. We wanted to create a similar thing, only for adults, fashionable, luxurious, and minus the hippo-on-hippo action.

We also figured that a coordinating world would be easily shoppable. We loved the idea that if you went into the store and picked out this pair of baby-blue pants, boom, you had a baby-blue T-shirt and cashmere sweater that matched it. We wanted to take the mystery out of putting together an outfit and be the stylists to the world. And although we didn't know what it was called per se, that skill was merchandising.

We looked back to the brands we lived in when we were growing up in the 1960s and 1970s, for ideas about everything from color and fit to trim and packaging. One brand was Dittos, which made Farrah Fawcett's favorite, high-waist jeans in dozens of bright colors, with saddle-back yokes to flatter the butt. Landlubber jeans were hip huggers with the perfect flared leg, and MacKeen jeans came with a collectable metal keychain attached, which girls used to wear like charms hanging off their purses. Another influence was LA designer Nancy Heller, who started her company in 1973 with buttery-soft, French-made T-shirts and later expanded into casual, colorful separates. Then there was New Hero, another amazing LA brand, founded in 1974, that made 100 percent cotton drawstring pants and matching tops with three-quarter-length sleeves and two strings at the neck that never tied. Those New Hero sets, which were as comfortable as pajamas, came in tons of colors, too.

In early 2000, we started playing with two different design concepts. One concept was a line of hip-hugging,

Dittos-like twill pants in bright colors that matched our T-shirts. And we really believed it was the one that was going to take us to the next level. But just in case, we had another concept—a line of terry-cloth tops and bottoms. We thought terry cloth was the most amazing 1970s fabric, and Gela had found the mother lode of terry-cloth inspiration while she was shopping like a maniac on that first trip to Japan. It was the T-shirt that changed history, as it turned out.

What she discovered in Japan was a whole visual world unlike anything she'd ever experienced. At the time Harajuku, the area around Harajuku Station in the Shibuya district of Tokyo, was the capital of street fashion, as featured in numerous street fanzines, including *Fruits*, launched by photographer Shoichi Aoki in 1994. In Harajuku, there was every kind of style you could imagine, and it was head-to-toe. The gothic Lolitas dressed in Victorian clothing, and the cosplayers as fictional characters from video games or anime. The visual kei kids were more androgynous, and the ganguro girls bleached their hair and wore extra-tan makeup, kind of like California girls on speed. Gela couldn't get enough of the insane ways the style tribes dressed, how they took fashion to the extreme and obsessed over brands and clothes in a cultish way.

Of course, there were stores to cater to every look, stores within stores within stores, and she was beyond inspired. The shopping bags were so cool that she brought them home for inspiration, too. One of the most amazing places she discovered was Burberry Blue Label. At the time, Burberry was still a staid, old-lady, nova check brand. But not in Japan. Burberry Blue Label was 100 percent owned by the Japanese, and they took Burberry and turned it into a Harajuku-style, girlie-cool brand with short plaid dresses and matching lipsticks and nail polishes—things that were so un-Burberry, but so Juicy. The whole fashion scene in Japan was enormously influential when it came to how we thought about the future of Juicy Couture, which developed its own cultish following.

But back to the T-shirt that changed history. It was the most killer mint-green terry-cloth tank top. Even better? It had the word "Maribu" written across the front, a misspelling of the most mythical of Southern California places, Malibu. We thought that shirt was the most brilliant thing we had ever seen, but it also happened to be the perfect 1970s Valley throwback piece. And it got us thinking about the possibilities of terry cloth as a clothing fabrication. Juicy Couture's philosophy was fit, fabric, and color. And terry cloth had a lot going for it where those things are concerned. Because it is a pile fabric, it took the dye in a way that was even yummier than the combed cotton we used for our T-shirts. And it draped beautifully. Also, what could be more luxurious than wrapping oneself in a buttery bath towel?

We believe that good style is comfort. Because when you are comfortable, you can have fun and express yourself. And when your feet hurt and your Spanx are going up your butt, you just want to go home. So we started playing with the idea of creating a terry-cloth uniform. At the time, the sweats that people were wearing were sloppy, oversize collegiate sweatshirts and sweatpants. It was true athletic wear with a men's fit. We went the other direction, giving those basics a sexy, body-conscious shape. It was all about an uber-flattering silhouette, kind of couture-esque really. And because we fit it on ourselves and we were super petite, our samples looked minuscule. In fact, when Vicki advised our sewers, she told them, "If you think they look like baby clothes, they are the right size." We designed a terry-cloth zip-up hoodie with front pockets that disguised your stomach pooch; narrow, set-in shoulders; and an hourglass silhouette that made your waist look as small as it could possibly look. The length was slightly cropped, so when the top was worn with the pants, it made your body look insane.

We were obsessed with every detail. At Almore Dye House, we learned that when we were dyeing our terry cloth, because it's a cotton-polyester blend, the reverse side of the fabric comes out looking mottled and heathered. It didn't take the dye the same. So we corrected that problem and paid a little more for a double-dye process to make the color sing. The first problem was solved: Hues were now candy-colored and vibrant, an Easter parade on acid. The second problem was the single-layer hood, which just didn't look finished. So we decided to line the hood with terry.

We wanted to make custom hardware for the hoodie,

because we have always thought that stock zippers looked cheap. We thought it would be chic to have some kind of charm or jewelry on the zipper pull, going back to the key-chain on those MacKeen jeans. And we have always loved the idea of monogramming, but couldn't do a "JC" charm, because that was already taken by Jesus Christ, ha! So we consulted Zabin Industries in downtown LA, which makes metal fasteners and embellishments. And they fabricated the J-pull that we designed, one that made the zipper uniquely G&P.

The J-pull was a genius bit of branding that became a status symbol even nine-year-old girls came to recognize. We used it to create authenticity about a brand that didn't exist before. That's what you want to do when you're branding something—create some extra detail to set your product apart. That J-pull zipper detail on our hoodies was our Polo pony, our Chanel "CC," and our Hermès "H" all rolled into one. It was recognizable from a mile away. It gave our tracksuits want-ability and became such a big deal that the National Cleaners Association of America had to issue a statement to its members about how to bag the tiny zipper pulls to protect them so they wouldn't fall off during the dry cleaning process.

We also made matching terry-cloth short-shorts, miniskirts, and pants. The pants sat low on the hips and had side seams that were cheated forward to make your legs look thin and long, and a flare at the bottom that was better than anything Dittos or Landlubber have ever come up with. We needed a waistband, so we dug into our bag of old tricks. Back when we started making "ICEE Juicy" logo tees, we also made matching little boys' underwear with "ICEE Juicy" silk-screened on the butt. Like the clear plastic backpacks, it was another one of our cheeky marketing projects and sly winks at pop culture. The little boys' underwear was for girls and the waistband had a Juicy logo like old-school Calvin Klein underwear. Think Marky Mark and Kate Moss. We sold a ton of that underwear as sleepwear. With market just weeks away, we still hadn't found the perfect waistband, and we were under the gun. So we used what we had. That elastic became the waistband for the terry-cloth pants.

Once the twill and terry-cloth groups were ready, Gela boxed up everything and sent it to Shaller's showroom in New York—everything except the terry-cloth pants, that is. Despite our best efforts, we both thought the pants weren't quite there. With the underwear waistband, they just didn't look finished.

Cut to Shaller in the showroom in New York just days before the resort market was scheduled to begin. Buyers were coming in to see lines that would hit stores in November 2000, in time for the warm-weather holiday travel season. Shaller started opening her boxes from us and was so excited about the terry-cloth zip-front hoodies she was jumping up and down. Then she got to the rest of it, picked up the phone, and let Gela have it. "What is this?" Shaller screamed. "I'm not going anywhere in that miniskirt or those short-shorts! They are one size bigger than my underwear! I want a goddamn pant!"

We put the pants in a box and shipped them to Shaller overnight. There wasn't time to fix the waistband, but we let it slide. We went with it and it was the right thing to do. You have to pay attention to your salespeople. It's an absolute key relationship in building a business, especially an apparel business.

And the terry-cloth tracksuits sold anyway. We were disappointed by the colors the stores chose—boring black, white, and red—because the colors were so exceptional (there was fuchsia and tangerine, too). But that was the same thing that happened when we started selling our T-shirts. It took a while for the Juicy colors to catch on. We also still felt the pants needed some tweaking. The basic silhouette was there. But that underwear waistband was so flimsy, it didn't hold up the pants when you wore them out. Our LA sales rep Joanne Fiske gave us her two cents: She'd be carrying groceries up the stairs, with her hands full, and by the time she got to the top her pants would be around her ankles.

So it was back to the design drawing board. Pam's son, Noah, was born August 4, 2000, and six weeks later, she was back to the Glitter Factory. She couldn't wait. The door of Unit G busted open and there was Pam with a baby carriage filled with everything you could imagine—toys, bottles, blankets. It was like Christmas had walked through the door. She had a giant comforter the size of a coffee table that she put down on the floor in the fitting room for nap time. It was a luxury, as an entrepreneur, to be able to take her son to work. We brought our dogs; we brought our babies. Work was our second home.

For the spring 2001 collection of terry-cloth pants, we decided to get rid of the underwear elastic and use a quick cord instead that we had used during our maternity days. Quick cord is a piece of elastic that has a draw cord inside, and it made the pants fit even better. We sewed the quick cord inside a two-inch, fold-over waistband, which really held in the muffin top. Fiske could carry her groceries up the stairs without fear. How did we know we had an idea that was worth sticking with and perfecting? All of us felt like there was something in that terry group, particularly the idea of having a bottom that went with a jacket so you could buy the full-blown set. So we stuck with it. Things take a while to evolve. And this was a faster evolution that most. In the end, once we responded to everyone's concerns, we got those pants right, and they changed the game. That's what collaboration is all about.

The tracksuit wasn't cheap to produce, or to buy—$80 for the pants and $75 for the top. It was an aspirational item that represented California luxury and ease. Your body looked good and you were comfortable, which was a winning formula. We didn't realize it at the time, but we were taking athletic wear and turning it into fashion at a time when women needed a uniform that would take them from the gym to lunch at Neiman Marcus, to their kids' soccer games. We gave it to them, first in terry cloth, and then, for fall, in velour, which draped well and took the dye in the same beautiful way that terry cloth did.

The tracksuit was well on its way to becoming a phenomenon. And then another key member of our growing family shuffled in our door like a ray of sunshine with boundless energy, drive, and an infectious giggle. Positive creative energy attracts like-minded people, and our Juicy team was becoming unstoppable. Janey Lopaty was a childhood friend of Pam's, a little pixie with a big mop of blonde Rastafarian hair. She didn't walk so much as she shuffled in these giant Spice Girls platform shoes. She loved fashion so much she would take off her clothes and try on things in the middle of a meeting, boobs a-flashin'. She's the most lovable person you'd ever meet. From the day she started working with us in August 2000, she lived Juicy Couture, she breathed it, she dreamed about it, and it was her life.

At her previous jobs, she had been working with VIP customers, first at the Tracey Ross boutique, and later at Stacey Todd. She sent boxes of clothes to celebrities so they could shop from home. It was called clienteling. And at Juicy, she turned it into a profession. Product placement is the way of the world now, and celebrities don't just expect to get clothes for free, they expect to get paid for wearing them. But lucky for us, we happened to be smack in the middle of the Hollywood community before celebrity fashion became pay-for-play. And it created a unique opportunity of which Janey took full advantage.

All the TV and movie costume designers were based in LA, and they were already pulling our clothes from stores. Bijou Phillips and Julia Roberts were buying them for themselves at Fred Segal. Our jeans were popular with celebs, too. But that was nothing compared to what Janey tapped into.

She had a connection at Creative Artists Agency, which wasn't as tenuous as it sounds. Her brother-in-law's brother was Rick Kurtzman, an agent whose clients included Gwyneth Paltrow and Charlize Theron. Gela was married to Duran Duran's John Taylor, who was traveling back and forth to England all the time and in the middle of that scene. And Pam's husband, Jef, was producing films and TV shows and working with Jessica Alba, Reese Witherspoon, and other Hollywood "It" girls. Between those connections, and our publicist, Lara Shriftman, we had access to quite a few people. And Janey was fearless when it came to working it. She found out people's sizes and sent out boxes of free clothes to them. Or, if she was at lunch sitting next to someone famous, she shuffled up to their table, introduced herself, and said, "Hi, I'm Janey from Juicy, can I send you a box of clothes?"

Back then, there were not a lot of fashion companies with warehouses in LA like ours, and Janey could get clothes to celebrities in an hour. She made it easy for them by sending a messenger service to their houses, or inviting them to come to our offices in Pacoima and pick out styles themselves. And they couldn't get enough of it. But we never paid them to wear Juicy. We may have given it to them for free, but they wore it because they wanted to and then they got photographed by paparazzi coming out of the Coffee Bean & Tea Leaf, or going to the gym or sitting at a Lakers game in their favorite Juicy Couture tracksuit.

Those photographs, it turned out, were worth millions of dollars in advertising. This was the time, at the turn of the millennium, when celebrities were becoming the new arbiters of fashion and style and LA was the capital of casual cool. New York–based glossies like *Vogue* and *Elle* were being challenged by celebrity style coverage in *Us Weekly*, *inTouch*, *Star*, and *People*. Celebrity looks showed up almost instantly across America, giving celebrity weeklies (and the brands they featured) an advantage over traditional monthlies with their long lead times. And more than a Gucci shoe, the items in *Us Weekly* and *Star* were accessible, and celebrities gave them validity. They tied into high fashion but were things, like a Juicy Couture T-shirt or tracksuit, that anyone could wear.

Seeing the way the world was changing, and that we were right in the middle of it in LA, Lara Shriftman proposed that we host a "day of indulgences" at the Chateau Marmont on July 26–27, 2001, not long after the new and improved Juicy tracksuit came out for the spring season. The Chateau Marmont, if you don't know, is a famous Hollywood landmark and Gothic-style hotel built on a hill above Sunset Boulevard in 1927 and known for hosting celebrities. Tons of writers and artists have lived and worked there, including F. Scott Fitzgerald, Dorothy Parker, Hunter S. Thompson, Jay McInerney, Sofia Coppola, Annie Leibovitz, and Bruce Weber; and, sadly, John Belushi died in one of the bungalows after a night of debauchery in 1982. It's always been the coolest hangout in town.

Lara explained that the event would be a celebrity suite and said that it would be a great chance to team up with a few other fashion and beauty brands, and to get our product into the hands of celebrities and tastemakers. The celebrity suite trend started in the early 1990s, when fashion and beauty brands set up shop in hotel suites around the Academy Awards, and are now a mainstay of awards show season, when designers, hairstylists, and cosmetic brands vie for media exposure that comes with the visit of a famous client. But we weren't so sure. It sounded like a lot of money: $50,000 to put on a party over two days and give away five hundred free pieces of clothing? And we were already getting our product into the hands of celebrities. But we thought about it and decided that it would be a nice thank you to our Hollywood clientele. More than that, it ended up being the perfect storm of celebrity and fashion.

Free clothes, beauty treatments, champagne, and a penthouse at the Chateau? What more could a Juicy girl ask for? We invited eighty guests, including Jennifer Love Hewitt, Rebecca Romijn, Mena Suvari, Tiffani Thiessen, Gisele Bündchen, and Sharon Stone. We offered them each a free outfit from our new spring 2001 line of terry-cloth tracksuits and short-shorts, as well as a chance to order from the fall collection of T-shirts, polos, corduroy and velour pieces, and our new cashmere sweaters. We also let people customize pieces, which was something Janey suggested after seeing the success she had had with monogrammed gifts at Tracey Ross. (Little did we know how successful personalization would become for our brand.) Stone ordered a cashmere hoodie with "Bronstein Rules" embroidered across the back, and jeans that read "Phil" on the front of one leg and "Roan" on the back of another in a reference to her then-husband, Phil Bronstein, and her son Roan.

It was the perfect LA day: sunny and warm, with a slight breeze blowing through the penthouse suite. Everyone we invited came and stayed. They tried on clothes, sipped champagne, and kicked back on the terrace overlooking Sunset Boulevard, where manicurists flown in from Buff Spa in New York were giving fabric manicures and pedicures, gluing tiny pieces of vintage Céline blouses and such onto nails. People hung out for hours. Farrah Fawcett said she wished she could have slept over! *Us Weekly* covered the event, running a two-page spread with photos of celebs in our "Viva La Juicy" T-shirts, shopping the racks, and lots of other magazines covered, too. It was fun, festive, and girlie, with lots of sweets and snacks, which is everything we love. And it was a social shopping experience. It became a model for countless other fashion marketing events in Hollywood.

Even if Hollywood isn't in your backyard, it's still important to get your product in the hands of friends and influencers, whoever those people happen to be in your community. Use whatever connections you have in whatever environment you're in, whether it's selling a T-shirt at your local shop or at a street fair or charity event, or giving hoodies to your friends to wear around town. The world is small—if your product is good, people will want to know where they can buy it.

After the response we got at that event, we were sure the tracksuit was going to take Juicy to the next level. We had created something wholly original, an instant classic, and everyone wanted it. For us, it was the right time, the right place, and the right product. And we were in touch with the right people. All the stars were aligned. But it took the village (of Hollywood) to get there. You can't succeed in a vacuum. It took a lot of little things—the terry-cloth T-shirt from Japan that started it all, Lisa Shaller's obsession with knit pants, Janey's love of all things Juicy, and Lara's off-the-charts celebrity suite—to create the perfect Juicy layer cake. Ultimately, it was the two of us who said yes or no, but we couldn't have done it without listening to the people around us and processing all that information. People think a successful business happens in a moment, an instant. But, no, it's a whole convergence of things, a snowball effect. It wasn't overnight. But once it hit, it was astronomical.

Taking It to the Next Level

Brainstorm other product categories that you could go into while still staying true to your brand DNA.

Concept a couple of ideas at one time.

Share them with your team, and listen to feedback about how they work in the real world. Then refine the details.

Find your J-pull. Once you have one winning concept for a new product category or extension, make it uniquely yours by giving it a recognizable feature or detail.

Timing is everything. You have to hit with the right idea at the right time.

The world can be a small place if your product is good. Give it away to influencers and tastemakers, or host an unforgettable event.

Chapter 7
The Tidal Wave

You can't set out to create something like the Juicy tracksuit. But if there is something you want to say, it can turn into that. Before Juicy, the vision of a girl in sweatpants was the ultimate in nonglamour and antifashion. But when we gave sweats a snug fit and buttery-soft feel, elevating them from sloppy to sexy, it flipped the switch and sent Juicy Couture into the stratosphere.

The Juicy tracksuit changed the way women dressed. It was a design of its time on par with Chanel's little black dress and Yves Saint Laurent's *le smoking* in the way that it captured the zeitgeist—the celebrity takeover of fashion, the casualization of culture and women's yoga- and Pilates-toned lifestyles—which is why in 2004 the Juicy tracksuit was inducted into the permanent fashion collection of the Victoria & Albert Museum in London.

The tracksuit was an attainable status symbol, a new urban uniform for first class *and* coach class that came on the scene at a time when the fashion and magazine publishing industries were discovering that celebrity sells. Having the right people in our clothes proved to be more valuable than any business plan or high-profile advertising campaign could have ever been at that point. What started as a cult LA brand quickly became mainstream. Because Juicy was affordable relative to other fashion brands worn by Hollywood actresses, you really could dress like your favorite star. When Hollywood wore Juicy, the world followed.

But no star in the universe could have sold Juicy if the product had not been good. Before the Juicy tracksuit, when you went shopping with your mom at Neiman Marcus, you were going in panty hose and a skirt. But our sweats were luxurious enough that you didn't feel like you were leaving the house with curlers in your hair. We created a new look that was comfortable but polished, with a style punch to take women from carpool duty, to the gym, to lunch with friends, and even to cocktails. If you didn't wear the whole suit, you could wear the pieces as separates. And many women did. At the four-way crosswalk on Rodeo Drive on a Friday afternoon, you'd see tracksuits at every corner, paired with the latest designer handbags and Gobstopper-size diamond rings. At Mr. Chow in Beverly Hills on Saturday night, you'd see the pants with a Chanel jacket and stilettos. At the movie theater in Westwood on a Sunday afternoon, you'd see a hoodie in every aisle. At the airport, in Middle America, at parent-teacher conferences, on college campuses, and at shopping malls, Juicy was the label on everyone's hips.

All the celebrity attention, coupled with the right product at the right time, turned into increased sales, demand, and growth beyond our wildest dreams. All of a sudden, Juicy was everywhere. It was a pop culture phenomenon. And at times, it felt like a tidal wave had hit us. But we had learned how to bob and weave, and we knew we could ride it out. A lot of times in business, people say you need to control your growth. We don't agree. When something hits, you have to figure out how to up your game to meet that volume, otherwise you peter out and somebody bigger and stronger than you will come in and kill your business with their ability to turn it out faster and cheaper. Our philosophy at the time was this: Have no fear, take no prisoners!

The tracksuit may have been the hit, but it was in good company. Juicy Couture had grown into a full-fledged casual lifestyle brand. We had hundreds of styles in the collection, including basic T-shirts, logo tees, polo shirts with embroidered Yorkie dog logos on the chest, cashmere sweaters, twill military jackets, blazers, motocross jackets, flippy linen skirts, shorts, wide-leg pants, dresses, corduroy hip huggers, and Juicy Jeans, plus scarves, hats, tube socks, and logo flip-flops. Everything came in the full Juicy palette, and it was selling as fast as we could make it. With

Hollywood's most beautiful women pouring their perfect bodies into Juicy, everyone else wanted to do the same.

Over the years, there were lots of celebrities who were good to us, and we were good to them. It was a mutual fan club. But it was also a well-oiled machine. Janey turned celebrity gifting into a business model by giving it her personal touch. She forged relationships with stars she thought would be good ambassadors for the brand and hand-selected pieces to send to each person. She knew Cameron Diaz loved the color blue, for example, so she would send her all the newest Juicy pieces in blue, and when the Golden Globes nominations were announced, she sent monogrammed scarves to all the Best Actress nominees. Janey also zeroed in on key items from each collection to send to stylists, including Andrea Lieberman, who worked with Jennifer Lopez and Gwen Stefani (Andrea is now a designer in her own right, with her own killer line of clothing called A.L.C.), and Patricia Field, who worked with Sarah Jessica Parker on HBO's *Sex and the City.*

The messenger service rolled up to our offices in Pacoima ten to fifteen times a day to pick up gifts going out to celebrities. Janey didn't bother with fancy boxes or ribbon. She just stuffed the clothes in shopping bags for easy access, with a note that read "Enjoy!" and a card with her phone number on it so celebrities could get in touch with her directly. She knew all of Hollywood's sizes by heart, and we had a wall of handwritten thank-you notes to show for her knowledge and dedication.

Over the years, Janey gave away thousands of pieces of Juicy, maybe even millions. She sent Juicy care packages to Jessica Alba and Halle Berry several times a month. Of course, celebrities could have passed the clothes along to their housekeepers and nannies and that would have been the end of that. But they wore Juicy and loved it. Sometimes, they would wear a piece a month later, or sometimes it would be the same day they received it. One time, Janey sent a scarf over to Halle, and she was photographed wearing it that very afternoon, when she picked up her kid at school. It was instant exposure for our brand.

Fashion directors at the celebrity weeklies like *People*, *Us Weekly*, and *Star* couldn't get enough of those paparazzi photos, which they sifted through on an hourly basis for their pages. There was Reese Witherspoon coming out of the Rite Aid in Brentwood in her lemon-yellow velour hoodie and robin's-egg-blue velour pants, Lara Flynn Boyle walking her dog in Malibu in her all-white suit, and Britney Spears heading to dance practice in the Valley wearing her blue tracksuit and Uggs. Valet stands and Starbucks parking lots were our fashion runways. And the magazines played their part, running regular photo spreads of Hollywood wearing Juicy, with headlines like "The Juicy Brigade" and "The Juicy Couture Fan Club." Bloomingdale's, Saks, and our other retailers got calls from women who wanted the same look. They couldn't keep Juicy in stock. Shipments sold out in one day and waiting lists formed.

Those paparazzi photos were such powerful sales tools

that they helped turn Juicy into a household name, just like the celebrities we were dressing. And not just in the United States. When Madonna married Guy Ritchie and moved to England in 2000, it was about the same time that Gela started spending a lot of time in England with John. Gela noticed in all the newspapers that the Brits had nicknamed Madonna "Madge," and told Janey about it. It turned out Madonna's stylist, Arianne Phillips, had already contacted Janey about tank tops for the pop star's backup singers. So Janey, who had specialized in monogramming gifts during her time working at Tracey Ross, decided to throw in a camel-colored terry-cloth tracksuit for Madonna with her nickname, "Madge," embroidered on the hoodie. Madonna was photographed wearing the tracksuit and it caused a sensation. "Madonna's Got a New Badge," one headline read.

When we saw the pictures, we were blown away. We had always loved Madonna, her drive, and her passion. She was a maverick who turned the music world upside down. She was a total style icon and fashion "It" girl, a real influencer. At that minute, it connected: Madonna knew who we were, she got us, and she was wearing Juicy! That photo traveled the world and was published hundreds of times in newspapers and magazines. All of a sudden, everyone wanted a personalized hoodie. We sent one to Cameron Diaz embroidered with "Cameron," one to Drew Barrymore embroidered with "Mrs. Green" (she was married to Tom Green at the time), one to Jennifer Aniston that read

"Mrs. Pitt" (her husband was Brad Pitt at the time), and one to Sarah Michelle Geller embroidered with "Freddie" for her fiancé, Freddie Prinze Jr. Then the girls started trading and wearing each other's hoodies, which created another flurry of media attention—and helped kick off a whole fashion trend for monogramming not only Juicy, but anything and everything.

Anytime someone got married, Janey made them a suit personalized with their new last name. We rode that wave for a long time, until we started realizing how many of those people to whom we'd sent personalized hoodies were getting divorced, and started to wonder if the hoodies were a curse! The curse of Juicy! (When Britney married Kevin Federline, they gave personalized sweatsuits embroidered with "The Maids" and "Pimp Daddy" to members of their bridal party, and many people probably could have predicted that union wouldn't last.)

Another version of the tracksuit that caused a media frenzy featured our "Juicy" name on an unconventional piece of real estate. The idea was innocent enough. In 2001, when Gela was with her son Travis at his seventh-grade orientation at school, she noticed a cheerleader wearing a pair of shorts with the word "Cheer" on the backside. She thought it was the cutest thing, so we decided to design track pants with the word "Juicy" across the posterior (and believe us, getting that "I" to sit just right took more than one crack). The pants were a huge hit at retail, but some parents objected, and some schools even went so far as to ban the pants. We even got letters from some parents complaining! We never thought of it as sexual because that's not how we think of the Juicy brand. We just thought it was another crazy nod to pop culture, like our "Viva La Juicy" and "Smells Like Couture" logo tees.

Every week, Janey hit the newsstand to find out where Juicy had landed. She'd shuffle in with a stack of magazines that weighed more than she did (the *National Enquirer* probably weighed more than she did). She'd clip out all the photos and bring them to us, then we'd post them on the wall for everyone to see. At our office, we had a wall of fame and a wall of shame. On the wall of fame was Madonna taking her kids to the park, Gwyneth grabbing a coffee, and J.Lo on her way to the gym. On the wall of shame were women in less flattering situations—Mariah Carey wearing Juicy during her much-publicized nervous breakdown; publicist Lizzie Grubman, who ran down a crowd outside a club in the Hamptons, wearing the tracksuit on her way to jail; and Gucci murderess Patrizia Reggiani, who was convicted of orchestrating the murder of her ex-husband, Maurizio Gucci, wearing a tracksuit at the funeral. We loved it all. We didn't care where you were going in the tracksuit; as long as you were going, we were happy.

Not only was the tracksuit on fire with celebs, but other styles were, too. Sarah Jessica Parker wore our strapless terry-cloth shirred dress in grass green in *Sex and the City* with Manolo Blahnik heels and an Hermès Birkin bag for the ultimate in high-low, casual luxe. Reese Witherspoon wore the pink tracksuit and had a Chihuahua sidekick when she played sorority sister–turned–legal eagle Elle Woods in the 2001 film *Legally Blonde.* Paris Hilton and Nicole Richie wore the tracksuits with Ugg boots on their reality show, *The Simple Life.* Foxy Brown called out Juicy on one of her albums, and Jennifer Lopez danced around in a Juicy bubblegum-pink velour hoodie and short-shorts in her 2001 "I'm Real" video, and loved it so much, she created her own version of the tracksuit for her label Sweetface. Later, when she was photographed wearing a canary-yellow linen caftan dress with crochet lace trim that we designed, Janey got two hundred calls about the dress in a single day. Stores sent the caftan dresses they had ordered back to us so that we could re-dye them in canary yellow.

The celebrity piece of our success was more organic than it sounds. We weren't friends with a lot of celebrities, but we were friends to them, and we wanted to help when they needed something. Some of them even came to our offices themselves. One night, the leggy Brazilian fashion model Gisele Bündchen came and got clothes for herself and all of her sisters. She was so gorgeous. She liked our cords because they were cut long and were good for tall people. It was not transactional like it is now, where you have to go through a manager, a publicist, and a celebrity stylist. Now it's "show me the money," but then, it was just friendly. Celebrities wore our clothes and knew they'd be photographed. It was exposure for them, too.

Even the New York–centric fashion establishment was

starting to pay attention. *W* magazine ran a full-page photograph of Reese Witherspoon in one of our cashmere hoodies with the J-pull front and center. This wasn't celebrity press in *Us Weekly* or *People*; this was a glossy monthly fashion magazine, and the stylist put Reese Witherspoon in Juicy Couture! We looked as good as any designers in that magazine. And it made our hearts pound.

Our publicist, Lara Shriftman, talked us into going to New York to have coffee with *Vogue* fashion features editor Sally Singer, who wanted to meet us. Pam was afraid of flying at the time. But to meet Sally Singer, it was worth downing a few greyhounds. No turbulence would keep her away from *Vogue*, which was our bible. We wanted to be in *Vogue* so badly we must have bugged Lara about it at least once a week. And little did we know what amazingness would come out of that meeting.

Sally was interested in us because she had recently written a story for *Vogue* where she traveled around the country to the biggest cities (including LA, San Francisco, Houston, New York, and Miami) to poll women about what items of clothing in their closet they couldn't live without. The one thing she heard in every city was the Juicy tracksuit. Our concept of soft dressing was resonating with shoppers because we were taking sweats out of the sportswear realm, turning them into fashion, and giving jeans a run for their money, and Sally wanted to come to LA to write about us.

Timing is everything. You have to hit with the right

idea at the right time, or it doesn't take off. It's not that no one had done a tracksuit before, but at that moment, everyone was ready to gobble up our particular concept of luxurious workout gear. It turned out they were also ready to try to get a piece of our success. By the end of 2002, we had competition from some of the biggest players in the fashion industry. Ralph Lauren, DKNY, Gap, and Victoria's Secret were all making sexy velour tracksuits. Some of our best stores, including Bloomingdale's and Neiman Marcus, had versions of them in their private-label collections. On the runways for fall 2003, designers all over the world, including Michael Kors, Jean Paul Gaultier, and Gucci's Tom Ford, mixed luxurious fleece separates or track pants into their collections. Big sports companies like Nike and Adidas were adding capri pants, fitted sweatshirts, and other fashionable styles to their lines, too.

The competition (and imitation) was flattering, but we didn't let it get to us. We thought, Bring it on! Imitation is the greatest form of flattery. If someone is copying you, that's good. Do the next thing. It means you are doing something right. People would walk into the office upset that Gap was knocking us off, but we didn't care. People are still copying Chanel's little black dress and Yves Saint Laurent's *le smoking*. It validates you. Besides, Juicy was the gold standard.

Back in Pacoima, our sales volume was creeping up from $20 million to $25 million, $25 million to $30 million, $30 million to $35 million. From 1998 to 2002, our sales grew fivefold, at a rate of more than 80 percent per year. It was massive growth. It was the boom time, which made for a very happy work environment. Every day was a "Hell yeah!" moment. The money and the love were a-flowin'. We reveled in a culture of fashion, family, and fun, all of which were cornerstones of our brand, and we always had lots of pets in our office to keep us company, including Dan, Pam's Yorkshire terrier, who traveled exclusively in a Louis Vuitton bag and inspired the Yorkies on our labels, and Tink, a Chihuahua who was tiny, cute, and vicious, and used to steal all the food off everyone's desks and drag it back to her carrier. All the girls at the office started getting dogs. There was even a miniature horse named Bucky who belonged to one of our patternmakers. Nobody wanted to leave their pals at home, so they brought them to Juicy camp, and it made us all want to stay longer and be more productive.

We were there for each other in good times and bad. On 9/11, we all stood in a circle in the warehouse and said a prayer. We told people they could go home and be with their families or stay with their office family if they felt more comfortable. And some of them stayed. It was an unimaginable tragedy that changed the world. Many of the boutique owners on Long Island we had been selling to since the early days lost family members. Even though we were in LA, and outside of the fray, it was terrifying. And we tried to do what we could to help. We had a T-shirt design in our line at the time with an American flag on the front that read "Made in the Glamorous U.S.A.," which was also our mantra and on our labels. We donated all proceeds of the sale of those shirts to 9/11 charities, and we recut the shirt four times.

On happier days, we functioned as a massive creative organism that tried on clothes all day long. We had about fifty people in the office by 2002. Sometimes, you'd come to work and change clothes so many times you couldn't find the shirt you came in wearing. And if you spilled something on your sweater, you could always go back to the warehouse and pick out something new. There was no corporate hierarchy. Everyone was on the same level and could speak up. We were a crazily tight-knit group of practical jokers who loved to get together at four P.M. and eat candy. Every day was a celebration because everyone wanted our clothes.

Understanding what your culture is and celebrating it is a big part of a productive workplace. You want the people who work for you to love coming to work every day. We had a Halloween pageant every year, and people went all out. We actually paid our employees $50 each to enter the costume contest. We closed the office at midday and started the festivities. We had great snacks (always): cookies and cakes and enchiladas. And there was every kind of candy, of course. When it came time for the pageant, it was like a Halloween version of *American Idol.* One of the members of our merry crew, Gerard Dislaire, a serious beauty whom we called "Frenchie," was the master of ceremonies, and always came with a trunk of clothes in case someone didn't have a costume. But that was rare. We had guest judges (John stepped in at least once), and the winners walked away with cash and prizes—good prizes, like washers and dryers.

One year Gerard dressed as Ziggy Stardust; another year he dressed as Andy Warhol. There were sample sewers who came as walking J-pulls and full-blown bunches of grapes. And one time, Bucky the miniature horse came as Shrek, dressed in a green tracksuit. It was hysterical! But not nearly as hysterical as when Diana and Marlena came dressed as the two of us, wearing long-haired wigs and throwing around a stuffed dog that looked like Dan and a baby doll that looked like Noah. We were laughing so hard we were crying. We always had a good sense of humor about ourselves. One for all, all for one.

The bigger Juicy got, the more Juicy people wanted. We had to keep feeding the savage beast and coming up with new product. Work begets work and success begets success. Once we were on a roll, it was easy to keep rolling. The ideas just kept coming, and enough of what we did was a hit that we had momentum. Sitting in a room, riffing off each other, was working. And when you start to have success with something like the tracksuit, it's encouraging.

We've always been enthusiastic consumers of fashion. You can't be in our business and not be. And we wanted to bring the same excitement you get from buying a Chanel jacket or Hermès bag to the casual world. Since we had a limited number of fabrications, working mostly in the parameters of terry and velour, and everything was garment-dyed, it helped focus our design process, and it made Juicy easy to understand as a merchandised collection. (Again, going back to our concept of no-brainer Garanimals dressing.) So if we were going to make a hippie dress, for example, it wasn't going to be in silk; it was going to be in terry cloth, which made it uniquely Juicy. There was always a nod to fashion, but in a casual, sporty, LA way.

We were responsible for designing everything, which was a major task. We'd meet with our patternmaker, Jan, tell her what we were into, and she'd do a flat, technical sketch. We suggested shorter or longer sleeves, hems, etc., and then she'd make a pattern. Once we saw the first sample, we'd try it on, pin it, and fit it to ourselves. Then Jan made adjustments. If you watch a documentary about how a designer works, often they will do a sketch with strong shoulders and beads here and there, hand it over to a workroom, and voilà! You have the whole collection. We did it our own way, by fitting samples on ourselves. We were very hands-on. That was our style. And it's how we built our business—at least in the beginning: just the two of us and a patternmaker.

We were designing eight collections a year, with a different color palette for each one. We had to make test fabrications, make sample collections, name dozens of new colors, and work with graphic designers on new Juicy slogans and logos. It was a lot, but we were having the time of our lives. And then we added more to our plates. Our personalities are such that we have always been enthusiastic about creating more and more product. (Two girls who love stuff, remember?) At the same time, we were hearing from our buyers that they wanted more. There's no easy way to know if the time is right for product extensions or new channels of distribution. You just have to look at your infrastructure, decide if it can take on more, and go for it—or not.

We launched Juicy Baby with mini-me versions of our colorful terry-cloth hoodies and track pants for girls ages two to six, as well as T-shirts with Juicyisms such as "Let Them Eat Cake" and "Princess of the T." It was a natural progression to do mother/daughter dressing, because our clothes were cut so small anyway, a lot of young girls were already wearing them. And all we had to do was essentially miniaturize the styles we were already doing for the women's line. Everyone in the family wanted something Juicy. And celeb moms like Kate Winslet, Uma Thurman, and Kelly Ripa loved it.

We also started to ramp up our international expansion. How we started selling in the UK is kind of a crazy story: One day, we just sent a box of Juicy to the buyer at Harvey Nichols in London with a note that read "If you sell it, we're in business. If you don't, it's a gift." Well, it worked, and by 2001, between Britain and Japan, our international sales accounted for 15 percent of our total sales. There was potential for even more, but we needed someone on the ground in Europe to shepherd our international growth.

We hired a woman named Amanda Lewis, a real self-starter based in London, to be the head of our international operations. She had worked at Helmut Lang and Alexander McQueen, and gave us a lot of valuable input. She told us our labels, which read "Have a Juicy Day Love G&P," needed to be cooler and more brand-appropriate, so we changed them. The new labels read "Juicy Couture" with the image of a Yorkie dog modeled after Dan on either side. She also told us that in Europe, it was better to market our brand as "Made in LA" than "Made in the Glamorous U.S.A.," which is exactly what we had been told in Japan when we launched Juicy Jeans. So that's what we did, we brought LA style to the world. That's a lesson in building a brand and keeping it fresh. You can't sit back on your laurels. Even if you're on top of the world, you can always make subtle, beautiful changes. We always wanted to make it better, and we were always moving.

In October 2002, we opened our first in-store Juicy Couture boutique at Harvey Nichols in London and did our first big in-store P.A. (public apperance). We were so excited! When we arrived, there was a line around the block. We were like, "Whoa! What are they giving away?" And it was us! It would have been the perfect day if one of us hadn't accidentally taken a sleeping pill instead of an allergy pill and kept falling asleep. It was an *Ab Fab* moment for sure.

We created some special Brit-themed logo and slogan tees for the launch. "God Save the Juicy," "All You Need Is Juicy," "Prince William Is a Fox," and "English Muffin" were a few of the choicest ones. And looking back on it now, all the brainstorming about slogan and logo tees was invaluable; we were creating the codes of our brand.

We have always loved English culture as much as California surf culture, and the two really came together in Juicy. That's how we think. It's not linear. We would never like straight surf or straight Anglomaniac. It's always been a big mash-up of crazy things, superlayered and eclectic. Just like we twisted the Hermès logo, we loved to play with heraldry. Juicy Couture had a family crest and a fairy tale, both of which started out as designs for T-shirts but ended up on packaging and products for years to come. The words of the fairy tale read like this, "Once upon a time in a land far, far away called Pacoima, there were two nice girls, Pam and Gela, who set out to create the perfect girlie collection. Juicy Couture swept the land and they lived happily ever after."

Back then, every day was a pinch-me day. The fairy tale had come true.

Coping with Growth, the Problem You Want to Have

When something hits, up your game to meet the volume, or someone bigger and stronger will come in and steal your thunder.

Don't change courses. Build on momentum.

Keep moving, reinventing, and improving—your labels, your packaging, everything.

If your infrastructure can handle it, spin out ideas for new products to meet demand.

Look for new channels of distribution.

But as your distribution grows, keep careful watch over how your brand is being presented and be your own advocate.

As you get bigger, don't forget where you started. You are still the customer, and your product should still have your personal touch.

Let your employees share in the success.

Chapter 8
Getting Your Ducks in a Row

In 2002, we went from $38 to $68 million in sales, almost doubling our business in a matter of months. Whatever was the new thing, we couldn't sell it fast enough. It was our moment. We were really starting to make money and enjoy spending it. On what? Fashion, what else!? We upgraded our diamond rings, bought matching Birkin bags, and ordered custom Manolos by the dozen. (Disclaimer: It was a different time.) Dressing alike had become part of our brand story, so we were also buying multiples of everything, whether it was Chanel jackets, J. Mendel fox-fur shrugs, even TSE cashmere sweaters (we preferred the shrunken fit of the kid-size sweaters).

We were having the time of our lives. But success comes with a lot of growing pains. They call them growing pains for a reason. They're natural, and you want to have them. But they aren't fun. If you are not classically schooled business people, which we most definitely were not, it would be impossible to have the perfect infrastructure in place ahead of time, before you know if your business is going to catch fire. But you can at least anticipate what kind of changes will take place and how to react.

The faster we grew, the more strain it put on our infrastructure. The cracks were starting to show. Every store in the world wanted Juicy. And we wanted to give it to them. But we had to learn how to deal with the issues that came with increased demand, including the complexities in manufacturing and distribution, the limitations of our team, when to say no, and, ultimately, how to get help.

At a certain point, as entrepreneurs, you have to figure out what your needs are and what keeps you up at night. If you are successful, you will hit a wall when you can no longer just trust your gut. That's where corporate management comes in. In 2003, we sold our company for $56 million plus an eventual $200 million earnout, and not a week has gone by since then that we have not been asked, "How did you do it?"

The first thing you have to know is why you are selling. For us, there were many reasons, beginning with staffing and logistical challenges we were facing because of our astronomical growth.

In late 2001, we took over the twenty-five-thousand-square-foot warehouse on Wentworth just across the street from our original space in Pacoima. The place was so huge, we joked we'd have room to host a roller-skating night there, and even had a name for it: Club Flippers. We thought, What are we doing here? We're never going to fill up this place. But by the time everyone had moved in, we had already outgrown it. We had to hang up our skates. Our staff was growing like crazy, from fifty people to one hundred to one fifty and more. It was a sewn-together quilt of knowledge, a weird amalgamation of experiences. It wasn't a top down–designed system. It was designed from the bottom up, which was the only way we knew how to do it. If we liked you, and we liked your style, you had a job. But at a certain point, that approach wasn't the best. At $30 million, you are one kind of business, but when you hit $40 million, some people can grow with you and some can't.

Although we were crazy profitable, the systems we had in place to run our business were archaic. We were still doing a lot of things manually. Elva Gonzalez, who ran the warehouse, was still keeping track of some of our merchandise by counting out hash marks on a piece of paper, while other stock was cataloged by computer. Things were not state-of-the-art like they should have been for the kind of gigantic orders we had to process and ship internationally. We were figuring out that we needed more specialized staff and software programs in place, maybe even an off-site warehouse facility.

Keeping up with production was becoming challenging, too. We were serious players at department stores by this time, selling in more than two hundred doors, and those stores were counting on our dollars. Juicy was helping to define a new category in retail known as "contemporary." Until then, the majority of the women's selling floor at department stores was taken up by "missy" and "bridge" clothing. We're talking dowdy-looking separates that were less expensive (and less exciting) than designer clothes. That started to change in the early 2000s, when brands like Juicy Couture, Katayone Adeli, Joie, and Theory began offering upscale casual sportswear that was cool enough to have designer cachet, but with more accessible price points. We were paving the way for today's successful contemporary designers, including Alexander Wang, Phillip Lim, and Tory Burch. As the contemporary market grew, the missy and bridge categories dwindled, and department stores expanded their contemporary floor space. Seeing the enormous potential of the market, Barneys New York began opening smaller freestanding stores featuring only contemporary collections, called CO-OP stores.

At Nordstrom, Saks Fifth Avenue, Bloomingdale's, and Neiman Marcus, Juicy was on what is called "automatic replenishment." That meant our stores had standing reorders whenever they sold out of something. We were getting reorders every day—and not small ones. (We were in a great position to be able to fill them, since our business was located in Los Angeles, where our products were all manufactured and garment-dyed. If we had been in Asia, we never would have been able to turn around reorders in a matter of weeks.) When we shipped those reorders, the clothes were selling out as fast as the salespeople could stock them on the shelves.

It was produce, produce, produce. We went from having raw velour and terry cloth on hand at all times for our tracksuits in quantities of twenty thousand yards, to quantities of one million yards. We were producing more than three hundred thousand tracksuits in a single month. (Seventy-five percent of our business was tracksuits.) To meet the demand, we had to use more factories, more dye houses, more cutting services, more everything, which meant more room for error. If we were making three hundred thousand units of a specific style, for example, we would have dozens of different dye lots. And sometimes, the tops and pants would end up coming out in two different blacks. Other times, pants would come in with legs two different lengths.

We tried to find a production manager to get on top of it all, but it was like trying to control raging waters! One guy we nicknamed Grasshopper, from *The Karate Kid*, because his voice was soft and all he ever did was spew nuggets of wisdom that turned out to not be so wise. After a few weeks, he hopped off into the sunset. Another guy tried his hardest, even referring to his staff as the Dream Team. It was hardly the Dream Team—more like the Bad News Bears.

Eventually, we landed our real Dream Team leader. Kwila Lee was her name, and she scared us to death. She was a tough, hardworking, no-nonsense Korean lady, five feet tall, with glasses, and always in a prim pantsuit. But she was fierce and loyal. She told us that if we hired her, we had to do as she told us and not interfere with what she decided was the right move. We slid under the table when we heard that. Even more painful, she told us we had to stop working with our contractor Angela Torti, whom we had been with since our early days in the T-shirt business, and find someone who could better handle our increased production volume. It was so brutal. "We have to work with Angela; she's like our mother!" we cried. But it was Kwi's show. We had to give her free rein. We were not good at change, but at this point, it was inevitable.

In the warehouse, Elva was up to her ears. So we hired someone to evaluate the efficiency of her team. He decided what they needed were some proficiency tests, starting with a basic math test. Not only was he misguided, he turned out to be biggest thief on the planet. One night, we found him loading up his van in the back of the warehouse. And he wasn't the only one. We discovered three big theft rings at the time, one of them with a full-blown store set up in a garage to ship Juicy Couture all around the world! We didn't file charges against any of them—we didn't want to—but we needed to get things under control. It was all becoming a little too real. We weren't playing dress-up anymore.

At the same time that we were tap-dancing as fast as we could to keep up with demand, we were also concerned about flooding the market. A lot of people wanted Juicy, but we didn't say yes to everyone. It felt good to be in that position. We wanted to keep our brand aspirational and make sure the product was presented in the right way. And we had many retail partners who did just that and had a like-minded vision. Not so Barneys New York. We had been selling to Barneys since the beginning, but things were not going so well. First it was the excessive charge-backs. (Barneys wanted a huge discount when our shipment came in one day late.) And then it was how the line was being presented in the stores. They said if we played ball with them and paid the charge-backs, when they rolled out the CO-OP stores, we would get our own Juicy section.

It never happened, and we got fed up. The next time the Barneys buying team came to see Juicy in the showroom in New York, we told Lisa Shaller to tell them they couldn't see the line. Eventually, we sold to Barneys again. But there's a lesson in knowing when you are in demand enough to be able to say no. Stores make you feel so desperate that you do anything—pay to contribute to salaries and bonuses for the sales specialists, pay money for charge-backs, pay money for a page in their catalogs. And then they do whatever they want with you, putting you in the corner one day or taking you off the floor altogether the next. There comes a point where if a store is treating you badly, like Barneys was us, you have to stop and say, "If you want to sell Juicy, it has to be on our terms as well. It can't only be on yours." It can be scary to say no, especially for a young designer. But you have to be tough, be your own advocate, and look out for your brand image.

Things were moving so fast, at times we felt like we were in a boxing match. It was boom, boom, boom, boom, boom! Something new was coming at us every day.

When you are part of a phenomenon, it's exhilarating, but it's also scary from a financial standpoint. We were self-financed, and that carries a lot of risk. We'd been through the LA riots, the Northridge earthquake, and 9/11, and had seen that businesses can lose their footing overnight. We were shipping $30 million-plus of product and needed a bare minimum of 50 percent ($15 million plus) for the raw goods and manufacturing fees to produce it. We were still using the same revolving line of credit we always had. We ran a tight ship, had no debt, we paid our bills on time, and put most of our money back into the business. And over the years, our bank saw how good we were at paying down our loans, and kept increasing them. We were at the same bank where we took out our first $75,000 revolving line of credit, and now we had a revolving line of credit for $15 million! That was a $15 million loan on our tiny shoulders. We didn't have that kind of money personally, but our business had that kind of inventory. We had reached a point where we wanted to take some risk off the table.

How did we know the financial climate was right to sell? We knew LA style was hot, hot enough that in April

2001, the $700 million New York–based sportswear behemoth Nautica Enterprises bought trendy LA jeans maker Earl Jean in a cash-and-stock deal for $86 million. That was major news for a small, LA upstart to be snapped up by a Seventh Avenue stalwart known for preppy, nautical-themed sportswear.

Like Juicy, Earl Jean was a young company, founded in 1996. With dark-rinse, high-grade, low-waist, boot-cut denim at $110 to $130, Earl Jean was helping to create a new premium denim category built on the same belief in casual luxe that we had. Husband-and-wife team Benjamin Freiwald and Suzanne Costas Freiwald had a small business, but it had big potential. The company was reportedly doing about $30 million in annual volume, but was growing fast, in double-digit increments. With the backing and sourcing capabilities of Nautica, they would be able to grow faster in the United States and internationally, including rolling out Earl Jean stores and other product categories.

The deal was attractive to Nautica because it was a move into the younger, trendier, higher-priced contemporary world. Asked by *Women's Wear Daily* why the deal was attractive to him, Earl Jean's Ben Freiwald said, "We took a lot of risk off the table. The reality was as the company grew larger, our day-to-day risk became bigger and bigger. That's a pretty big motivator. The key was we felt the brand needed to go to the next level and we needed help with that."

When we read that, it sounded all too familiar. We had similar objectives to the Freiwalds: we wanted to take some risk off the table, and we were excited by the prospect of what Juicy could become with an influx of cash and infrastructure. Shoes, accessories, having our own stores—we wanted it all. It was time to start getting our ducks in a row to sell.

There are a lot of things you need to do to prepare to sell your business, and the whole process took us more than a year. First we met with our accountant, who gave us a blueprint for how to move forward, beginning by telling us that we needed to file paperwork with the IRS to change our company from an S corporation to a C corporation. (C corporations have no restrictions on ownership, but S corporations are restricted to no more than one hundred shareholders.)

Since we didn't always keep the most professional-looking records, he also recommended that we hire forensic accountants to get all our financial documents in order. Those poor guys, they came to our offices in Pacoima to look at our files, which we stored in the warehouse on a shelf under T-shirts in a box from Staples. Instead of a safe-deposit box, we kept our really important legal papers in an orange Hermès box, figuring we'd remember to grab it if there was a fire! We kept luggage in that nasty warehouse, too. It was like our garage, our home away from home. They said, "Um, you might want to do some cleaning up." But the *business* was clean, and that was what mattered. We had always budgeted like housewives. Our margins were insane (75 percent, because we had next to no waste), and we had very few operating costs and no debt.

The next step was to meet with potential brokers, the bankers who would sell our company. The first bankers we met with were from a big firm in Encino. It was just the two of us in a big conference room full of suits, and it couldn't have gone worse. They were completely dismissive. The guy in charge said, "My wife likes your tracksuits, but we're not interested." He said, "Nobody is going to buy your rinky-dink company because it is too small. You need to be at least a $100 million business before anyone will even look at you!"

We held it together, stomped ourselves and our matching Juicy baby-doll tops and trouser jeans back to the car, and started crying—and laughing. It was shocking to hear them talk to us like that. But we didn't let it get us down. We were young and brash and we weren't going to take no for an answer. It was, "Bullshit, baldy! Thirty million means something and don't tell us it doesn't. We're on top of our game and then some!"

The next name on our list was SAGE, the firm that brokered the deal for Earl Jean. SAGE Group was barely seven months old, a boutique investment bank founded by Mark Vidergauz and five partners who were trying to establish themselves as go-to guys for handling mergers and acquisitions in the $50 to $100 million range. (Most large firms, as we had learned in Encino, wouldn't even look at deals for less than $100 million.) Earl Jean had been their first big success. The SAGEians, as we liked to call them, were young and hungry (so young, in fact, that some of the guys who went around brokering deals weren't even old enough to rent cars). They were like us. They wanted companies like ours. And when we met with them, we immediately felt at ease.

We negotiated what percentage of the sale they would take (1.4 percent) and signed a contract. We had found our deal makers, now it was time to find our deal.

To come up with an asking price, SAGE began the process of preparing a business valuation, or a realistic idea of Juicy's worth and its projected rate of growth. They based their calculations on multiples of net income. Earl Jean's price had been based on a multiple of six, and that's what we wanted. Our businesses were almost the same size, and we wanted to sell for $86 million, too.

Once the SAGEians had completed the valuation, they put together a package to get preliminary bids. We had two options: to sell outright, or to sell part of our business to a private equity firm but retain majority (at least 51 percent) ownership. We entertained offers of both kinds. In the beginning, SAGE showed us a big list of potential buyers. But when it came right down to it, it was a much smaller pool, about four major players. So we packed our best Juicy and went to New York for the courtship process. We thought the corporate boardrooms on Seventh Avenue were boring as hell and the suits were complete and utter Martians. (And they probably thought *we* were Martians, too.) We went into those big meetings, saying, "Oh my God, isn't Juicy the most amazing thing in the world? Don't your wives and daughters just love Juicy?" We thought we had the biggest company the world had ever seen. We had an innate, weird confidence. We drank the Kool-Aid and expected they had, too. They wanted to talk about our numbers, but we just wanted to talk about our dreams.

We met with representatives of the private equity firm Saunders, Karp & Megrue, who had recently acquired a minority stake in Tommy Bahama, and thought there were similarities between the faux-island-lifestyle brand and Juicy. We had one drunken dinner with them at an Italian restaurant on the Upper East Side, where all they could talk about was "Tommy time!" which in their corporate lingo was a reference to happy hour. We couldn't take them seriously because to us, Tommy Bahama shirts were bad Christmas gifts. The poor SAGEians—one of them had total acid reflux and was guzzling Mylanta. He was like the parent embarrassed of his kids.

Saunders, Karp & Megrue ended up making an offer that would let us retain 51 percent control, but it would have been up to us to make key hires to grow our business. The problem was we never had time to sit back and look at the bigger picture. We were seriously out of control with our growth rate and hanging on for dear life. We didn't just need money, we needed smart money. We needed a partner, a big conglomerate with resources that could help us grow.

We met with Dickson Poon, the Hong Kong–based CEO of Dickson Concepts. Poon, who was educated at a British boarding school and in Los Angeles at Occidental College, started out in business with a single watch store in 1980, and parlayed it into an empire by securing the rights to sell Ralph Lauren, Perry Ellis, Escada, Bulgari, and other brands in Southeast Asia. In 1991, he bought (and turned around) the luxury British department store Harvey Nichols. We thought he was an interesting prospect, but in the end, his bid was too low. Plus, in our hearts we wanted to go with an American company, since we had "Made in the Glamorous U.S.A." proudly displayed on our labels.

The two biggest American players were Jones Apparel Group and Liz Claiborne, both billion-dollar fashion conglomerates listed on the New York Stock Exchange with impressive portfolios of companies that could be key resources for us when it came to consolidating supply chains and introducing new product categories. Jones, founded in 1975, had a license to produce the Lauren by Ralph Lauren sportswear line and owned the Gloria Vanderbilt denim brand, Nine West shoes, and branded jewelry manufacturers.

When we met with Jones CEO Peter Bonaparte, he almost broke our hands with his strong grip. We had never done so much handshaking in our lives. He thought the tracksuit was a fad, and that it was going to be over in a minute. He didn't see Juicy's lifestyle potential. Jones passed, but Peter told us later it was his biggest mistake. (He's a dear friend now, by the way, and a true fashion visionary.)

The first meeting at the corporate headquarters of Liz Claiborne was even more memorable. Now, Liz Claiborne might have been what we would call a "missy" brand, but it was one of the most successful American conglomerates on the scene at the time. And we respected Liz Claiborne the designer as a pioneer. Frustrated by the apparel industry's failure to make an affordable stylish uniform for the emerging female workforce, she started her own business in 1976, and her brand became the first one started by a woman to make the Fortune 500 list. Although she retired in 1989, when we visited in 2002, her office was just as she left it: filled with her wonderful collection of bonsai trees. As soon as you walked in the front door, it was pointed out that these were Liz's bonsais, and we thought that was very cool and respectful. Even with Liz gone, the company was still a very empowering environment, and creative in its own way. When you opened the door of the bathroom, you were hit with a spritz of the Liz fragrance Curve.

Chief executive officer Paul Charron, who joined the company in 1994, was a visionary, too. He was widely respected for broadening Liz's reach, and bringing it into the modern day by making strategic acquisitions such as Lucky

Brand and Laundry by Shelli Segal, both of which were young, trendy brands based in LA. Liz Claiborne also had an in-house fragrance department headed up by Art Spiro, and a group accessories division headed by Ed Bucciarelli, both of whom were forces in their fields and could be invaluable resources for us.

Still, everyone was so buttoned-up we weren't sure how we would fit in. We couldn't believe how quiet it was in the building. The place was like an echo chamber for our constant giggling and carrying on. We were convinced we wanted to sell for $86 million, and when we were waiting for everyone to arrive in the boardroom, we went around opening all the doors and cabinets and whispering to ourselves, "Is it in here? Is the eighty-six million in here?" We knew Liz had the cash, and the stock was doing well. Then we met Angela Ahrendts. Just forty years old at the time, she was a rising star in the business world who was senior vice president and group president of Liz Claiborne's modern brands, and went on to become the CEO of Burberry and now head of retail at Apple, and is one of the most suffcessful female executives in the business world. We thought she was the most aggressive, dynamic, amazing, intense person we'd ever seen. We wore white Dolce & Gabbana pantsuits to try to impress her, and she noticed them. We had found someone in the crazy corporate world who we could relate to. During that first conversation, she turned to us and asked, "What is your dream?" And we said, "We want to rule the world." Angela loved that kind of attitude. A lot of people sell their businesses, cash out, and go away. We hadn't even begun.

The whole courtship process lasted four to six months. Then it took another four months to get solid offers. A couple of the interested parties came out to LA to tour our offices. When Paul Charron came out he got lost on the way from the airport (like anyone would trying to get to Pacoima). We were all sitting there waiting like the principal was coming. When he finally did arrive, he couldn't have been nicer, even though we were trying to speak in different languages. He said, "Now tell me about your IT platform." And Pam said, "Is that a shoe?" He said, "Do you have a problem with shrinkage?" And Gela said, "Oh no, our shirts are garment-dyed, not piece-dyed." By "IT platform," he meant our computer systems, and by "shrinkage," he meant the financial accounting term for loss of merchandise between point of manufacture and point of sale. It was a clash of cultures—ours fly-by-the-seat, gut-driven, and entrepreneurial, and theirs spreadsheet- and bottom line–driven corporate. Clearly, we had a lot to learn.

Luckily, he got a kick out of us. Paul was a fatherly guy and a remarkable leader, and Angela was the mentor we needed to kick things into high gear. We loved chief operating officer Michael Scarpa, especially his Tom Selleck mustache. These people had moral compasses, and even if we didn't speak the same language, we had the same values. They took time out to meet every person on our team. And finally, they made an offer. The sale price would be $56 million, and whatever profit we made after the sale would be split thirty–seventy with Liz Claiborne. As part of the agreement, we had to give them two licenses, for fragrance and accessories. The deal was structured so that we would remain as copresidents of Juicy Couture. We had to hit certain sales goals in 2003, 2005, and 2007. Each time we hit the goal, we got another portion of our earnout money. (We hit every goal post, eventually making $200 million before we left.)

We could see that Angela and Paul were guiding forces, and Liz had a lot to offer, including a billboard in Times Square and lease agreements on retail streets we never would have been able to get on our own. We signed a letter of intent to accept their offer, and entered the due diligence phase, during which they had an opportunity to inspect our books, records, and assets. Because Liz Claiborne is a public company, we couldn't tell anyone what was going on, which was hard, because at the office, we had always had an open-door policy. And now our door was closed and men in suits were walking through all the time. We begged them to be less conspicuous. "How about jeans?" we said. Again, it was a clash of cultures.

Of course, during this time when we were supposed to be hush-hush, the media was more interested in us than ever because of the volume of tracksuits we were selling. In late 2002, a CNN financial reporter came to our warehouse to interview us. It was the first time he had ever covered anything in the world of fashion, and he asked us the most insulting question. "What do real designers think of you?" Our jaws fell on the floor. We said, "Huh? We *are* real designers."

Then, as if on cue, one of the girls yelled from the office that we had a phone call from *Vogue* magazine. It was Sally Singer, the reporter who had come out to LA to write a story about us. She was calling to say that *Vogue* editor in chief Anna Wintour liked the story, but wanted more. Anna wanted *Vogue* to take Juicy Couture to meet the real couture. "How do you feel about going to the haute couture shows in Paris?" Sally asked. We jumped for joy in our high heels and screamed so loud, they probably heard us all the way to Malibu. "We've won the golden ticket," Gela said.

We scurried our high heels back to the warehouse, where the CNN reporter and his cameraman were waiting and said, "Ha! What do real designers think of us? We're going to the haute couture shows with *Vogue* magazine, that's what they think!"

When the SAGEians found out we were going to Paris in January 2003, just weeks before the sale was scheduled to be finalized, they were worried. They said, "You need to focus on the sale." But we said, "Are you crazy? We're going to the couture! We'll deal with that later."

We felt like we'd won the lottery. But the lottery was going to the couture, not selling the business. That didn't feel real yet. We were so excited, we told Sally we'd book our own plane tickets and hotel rooms and she said, "No, no, *Vogue* is going to take care of everything: the tickets, the hotel, the show invitations. We're even going to arrange a party for you. And we're going to ride along on your excellent adventure for the magazine."

All we needed to worry about was a last-minute bit of homework we had to do for our new partners at Liz Claiborne. But more important, we had to worry about what we were going to wear.

Unit G, our first offices in Pacoima. Not glam, but they got the job done.

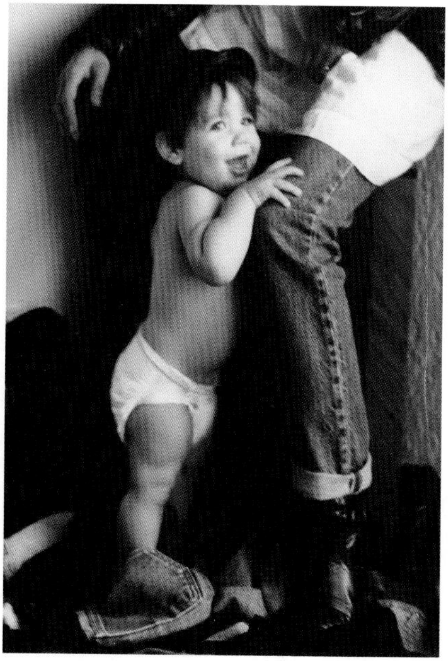

Our first Travis Jeans hangtag, 1990, starring the real Travis, our mascot for many years

Davis Factor

Our first maternity model, Sandra Bernhard.

Early accounting and the famous orange box.

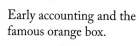

All images courtesy of the authors unless otherwise noted.

The shirt that prompted our first cease and desist from Hermès in 1999. Now this type of design is commonplace, but back then no one had ever done it.

Limited edition Pam and Gela Barbies issued in 2004 by Mattel.

Pam and Gela as Grace Coddington and Anna Wintour.

Dimitrios Kambouris

At the Met Ball in 2005 with husbands John Taylor and Jefery Levy.

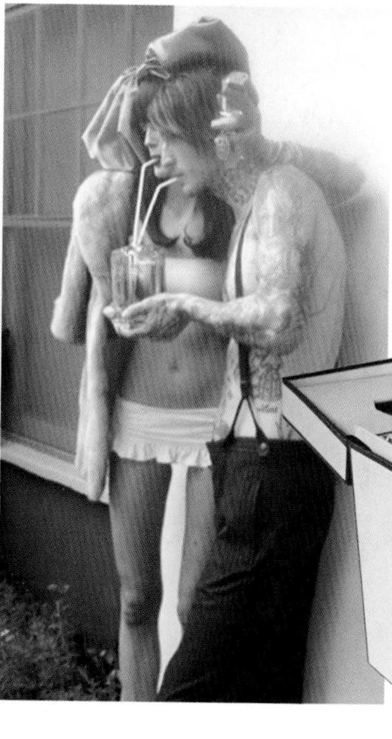

The first Juicy Couture fragrance, released in 2006, and an outtake from the fragrance ad campaign.

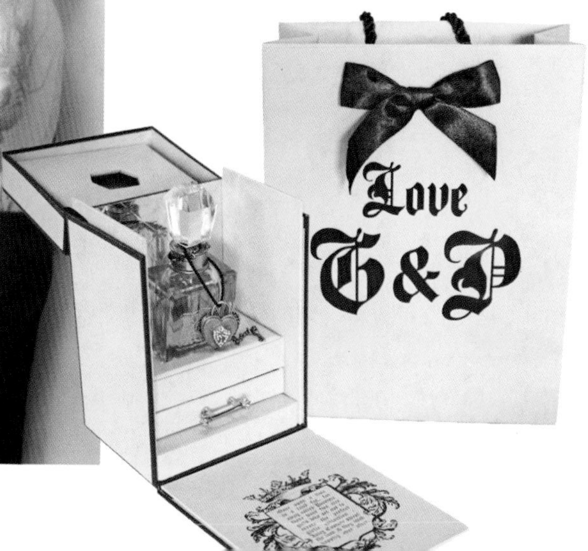

Getting ready for the Fifth Avenue flagship store opening in 2008.

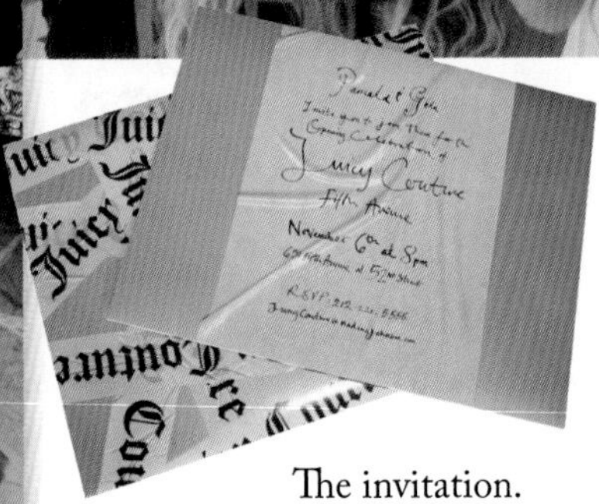

The invitation.

Our Juicy Couture Fifth Avenue opening party.

Donato Sardella

With Anthony Kiedis.

Halle Berry.

For every party we dressed up boys in G&P outfits. Martha Stewart loved the party and took a lot of photos and blogged about it. We were thrilled.

The Rodeo store opening party.

Images courtesy of Donato Sardella

Our beautiful fragrance campaign shot by Tim Walker and the most creative creative director, Robert Lussier.

Our signature Juicy dogs. They are real dogs. Dog lovers everywhere fear not: No dogs were harmed; it was vegetable dye.

Images courtesy of Tim Walker

The finished ads.

Tim Walker

One of our iconic Tim Walker ads.

The Fifth Avenue storefront.

Growing Pains: What to Expect

If you are successful, you will hit a wall where you can no longer just trust your gut. That's when corporate management comes in.

Some of your employees will be able to grow with you and some won't have the skill set to handle the increasing complexities of the business. You will need more specialized staff.

The cracks in your infrastructure will start to show and you will need more highly developed systems for production, distribution, and loss prevention.

Demand will outstrip the capabilities of your original contactors and manufacturers.

You will need more capital and know-how to reach the next phase of growth, whether that means opening stores, financing ad campaigns, or doing something else for your business.

The financial burden on your shoulders will keep you up at night.

You will want to take some risk off the table. That's when you start thinking about selling your business (or chugging tequila)!

How to Prepare Your Business to Sell

Look around you for a road map. Is the financial climate right? Have other companies like yours been sold recently and who were the players involved and the terms of the deals? You may want to reach out to the same players, including investment bankers and prospective buyers.

Meet with your accountant to get a blueprint for moving forward. You may need to file paperwork with the IRS and change the tax structure of your business to make sure it's favorable for a sale.

Get your financial records in order, and hire someone to help if need be.

Interview prospective investment bankers to broker the sale. Like anyone you hire, make sure they have a genuine interest in your success. Sometimes small is better.

Negotiate the percentage of the sale the investment bankers will get and sign a contract.

Work with investment bankers while they prepare a business valuation, or a realistic idea of your company's worth and its projected rate of growth. They typically base their calculations on a multiple of projected income.

Once they have completed the valuation, they

will put together a package and you can start entertaining preliminary bids.

Weigh your options for ownership structure. Decide if you want to sell outright or sell part of your business but retain majority ownership. In the end, we decided to get the resources we needed, and it was better to sell outright to a big corporation.

Enter the courtship process. Meet with prospective buyers and listen to what they have to offer in terms of infrastructure, development opportunities, and expertise.

Evaluate final offers. Again, trust your gut because this is someone you're really getting into bed with.

Chapter 9

The Couture Goes to the Couture

Being invited to the spring haute couture runway shows in Paris in January 2003 was beyond anything we could ever have imagined in our fairy tale thus far. It was like we were Cinderella and we were going to the ball! Except that it was way better than being Cinderella, because *Vogue* magazine editor in chief Anna Wintour was our fairy godmother.

Vogue was rolling out the Juicy pink carpet for the week—front row, backstage, we were the stars. They were getting us invitations to all the runway shows, including Chanel, Dior, Jean Paul Gaultier, and Givenchy, and arranging for us to meet every designer. They were planning fun diversions, too, including shopping trips to Paris's super-high-end vintage boutique Didier Ludot and the Paris flea market, and a tour of Parisian nose Frédéric Malle's perfume boutique. They even arranged to give us a party, which was hosted by none other than fashion's preternaturally tanned emperor himself, Valentino, and his partner, Giancarlo Giammetti, whose lifelong personal and business relationship was touchingly portrayed in Matt Tyrnauer's 2008 documentary film, *Valentino: The Last Emperor.*

Vogue's fashion features editor Sally Singer and European editor at large Hamish Bowles were going to be our tour guides, and they wanted our reactions to this rarefied world for a *Vogue* story, which would be published in the March issue. We were excited, but also a little nervous. What if no one took us seriously—or worse yet, if these designers of the most exquisite creations in the universe were dismissive of us for turning the world into tracksuit-wearing slobs?

Haute couture, which translates loosely to "high fashion," is clothing created by hand for a specific customer. It is made-to-order with repeat fittings, out of the most expensive fabrics in the world, with detailed hand-beading and embroidery. Juicy Couture was the polar opposite—tracksuits and T-shirts for all. A one-of-a-kind couture dress could cost as much as a car ($50,000 or more) and take up to three hundred hours to make. We were selling more than three hundred thousand Juicy Couture tracksuits every month at the affordably luxurious price of $160! We were designing a casual uniform that women could make their own—and spoofing the world of couture while we were at it. But Sally assured us, "People are going to love you." And she seemed genuinely interested in how our two worlds—fashion's past and fashion's future—would intersect.

The haute couture tradition dates back to Charles Frederick Worth, a nineteenth-century Englishman-turned-Parisian who was the first to put labels in his clothing and become famous around the world as a prestigious designer. He opened his business in 1858 and quickly gained a wealthy following, catering to the fashionable celebrities of the day such as actress Sarah Bernhard and French Empress Eugenie. Clients came to his house, or *maison*, in Paris to see his work on models in fashion shows, just as a patron might visit a painter's studio. Thanks to Worth, dressmakers were no longer considered mere artisans: they were artists with vision. Instead of having women dictate their own designs, as had previously been the dressmaking practice, Worth dictated how women should dress and the world followed.

Under his leadership, Paris haute couture became a luxury business governed by specific rules and regulations. In 1868, the Chambre Syndicale de la Haute Couture trade association was created to guard the designation of "haute couture." To be haute couture creators, designers had to conform to rules involving the number of designs made for day and evening wear each season, all of which had to be sewn by hand, by French employees, in French ateliers. (The term "haute couture" is protected by French law, but the term "couture" is not.) Only the best could qualify. And at the height of haute couture in the mid-twentieth century, there were more than one hundred haute couture houses. But with the rise of ready-to-wear clothing, the number of designers who qualify as couturiers has dwindled. Today, there are fewer than a dozen couture houses in France. Although the work has largely disappeared in the modern era of democratic design, the twice-yearly couture collections are still considered the creative laboratory for new ideas in fashion. And we couldn't wait to see what our favorite designers had dreamed up.

We had never been to a runway show, but it's not as if we were total strangers to the world of Paris fashion. Designers John Galliano, Alexander McQueen, and Karl Lagerfeld were our idols, so much so that we had pictures of their runway creations on our inspiration boards back at our dingy offices in Pacoima. Forget about bands, forget about actors, and forget about royals. We were full-on designer groupies. We followed their work religiously through the outrageously expensive trade magazine *Collezioni*, which was the only way to see every look in every runway show in the years before online sites such as Style.com came along. Not only were we fans of designers' works, we were obsessed with their fantasy lifestyles, too, and how they cared about the tiniest luxuries. (When we saw a TV show featuring the red cushions on Valentino's yacht, which he had monogrammed with his parents' initials to honor them, we were hooked. We knew what it was like to obsess over something like that in our own way. When we had dinner parties, we would fold and hand-stamp each place card with guests' names.)

We were such fashion groupies that we sent Juicy Couture tracksuits and T-shirts to all our favorite designers as gifts. For Galliano, we sent a shirt that read "King of the Fucking Universe" and for McQueen, "McQueen of the Fucking Universe." We had no idea if they wore them or not, although we did hear rumors that Galliano liked to go jogging on the Seine in our velour track pants, which dragged really long in the mud and ripped—and we thought that probably made them look even cooler.

When it came time to go to haute couture fashion week, we packed every goddamn thing we owned—Chanel for the Chanel show, Dior for the Dior show, Gaultier for the Gaultier show, check, check, check. We wrote down every outfit for every day, and color coordinated. We did a black color story and a beige color story. We had it all planned out, with lots of Juicy T-shirts and track pants to mix with our designer pieces because that was our view of the modern way of dressing. When it came to luggage, it was Louis, Louis, and Louis—Louis Vuitton, that is. We were so fashion- and label-happy back then. It was gangster central. The ice was flowing. We were mental—a cuckoo combination of new money and crazy LA.

When we arrived at LAX in our velour tracksuits, with

Hermès Birkin bags and eye masks in tow, we started our preflight ritual—buy magazines, gum, and Chex Mix, hit the airline lounge bar, drink heavily, and pop sleeping pills. Pam was the mixologist, pouring the vodka and grapefruit juice and stirring up the greyhounds. Before we got on the plane, we were determined to finish our homework for the Clairbornians, as we were now calling them. They wanted us to come up with a two-year business plan for international expansion with annual sales projections for every country. So we pulled the spreadsheet out of our pink "Choose Juicy" folder, and started going down the list of countries, some of which we'd never even been to. We're like, "Sweden—two million!" "Germany—four million!" We were high on life and joyful beyond. Besides, how could we have possibly been serious about projecting sales in Scandinavia? We called it our "greyhound budget." We didn't think they were going to hold us to it. But the Claibornians made us stick to that budget we did when we were drunk off our asses, and we ended up exceeding it by a lot.

Somehow, we managed to stumble onto the plane and notice an Academy Award–winning actor sitting behind us. He said, "I know you girls." (We had sent him clothes.) "And it looks like you probably have something that could help me sleep." We gave him one of our sleeping pills and he passed out so hard, he didn't wake up for the entire twelve-hour flight. We thought that might be his last performance. We really thought he was dead and we were going to be on the cover of *People* magazine for killing him.

Vogue put us up at the Hôtel Costes, a boutique hotel in the tony first arrondissement of Paris. The place was trendy beyond belief, smoke-filled and so dark you could barely see your hand in front of your face, much less a mirror to put on your makeup. There was no way we were going to be camera ready coming out of this place. But we didn't care. When we got to our rooms, it was heaven. Sitting on the desk was a mixed bouquet of exceptional flowers, a giant box of Ladurée macarons, and a stack of perfectly calligraphed invitations to the fashion shows. We had never had macarons from the historic Paris pâtisserie Ladurée, founded in 1862, and everything about them was exquisite—the pastel green boxes with gold lettering, the crisp gold-crested tissue paper lining, the pale colors of the delicious, double-decker, meringue-filled confections . . . It was the most gorgeous presentation we'd ever seen, and it inspired how we thought about product and packaging for years to come.

As it turned out, there was so much about that Paris trip that inspired us aesthetically. It was the start of a love affair with new people, places, and things. We were in the big leagues. But there wasn't much time to savor the moment right then. We were expected at our first show, for Japanese designer Yohji Yamamoto, in a few hours.

The Yohji show was a personal high for Pam. His avant-garde spirit had always appealed to her punk-rock mentality, ever since she first laid eyes on her future husband, Jef, in a Yohji Yamamoto trench coat at the LA restaurant Sushi On Sunset in 1989. Yohji was the coolest thing around in the 1980s and '90s, when Japanese designers first hit the scene in a big way. Pam got married in a three-piece white Yohji kimono dress, and Jef wore a Yohji tuxedo. And the runway show did not disappoint. It was held in an industrial warehouse in Paris, and we sat on the most uncomfortable rickety wood folding chairs. But it was worth it to see Yamamoto's minimalist extravaganza, even if we were by then maximalists all the way. The clothes were all deconstructed Edwardian silhouettes in houndstooth checks, beautifully draped in shades of black, white, and red. It was totally art damaged and so supercool.

The cast of exotic characters off the runway was just as wild. Now it's all celebrities paid by the designers to sit in the front row and attract media flashbulbs. But back then, it was still clients and industry insiders. Among the handful of ladies from around the world who could afford these one-of-a-kind creations, there was Deeda Blair, the Washington, DC, philanthropist and socialite, with her signature gray bouffant flip. She was wearing a brown crocodile jacket with the long, reptilian tail hanging down her back. Then there was Kal Ruttenstein, the late fashion director of Bloomingdale's, in his silver sneakers and Adidas track pants (he knew what was what!). And Carine Roitfeld, the French *Vogue* editor whom we'd had a girl crush on for as long as we could remember, with that mussed-up, postcoital glow only French women can manage. There was a hierarchy to who got to sit where, and we were front-row, baby! People were grousing about how late the show started, and having to wait so long. But we were happy just to be there. We weren't jaded.

The Chanel show was held at Ledoyen, one of the oldest restaurants in Paris, in the gardens of the Champs-Élysées. We wore matching brown tweed, fur-collared Chanel miniskirt suits with Burberry boots and Juicy tees that read "Rebel Couture." In the lobby, the eccentric British journalist Isabella Blow, dressed that morning in a black mask and cape, spotted us and squealed, "Here come the Juicys!" And that moniker stuck. People in the press then started calling us the Juicys. Blow was famous for her outrageous outfits. Later in the week, she was booed by guests at a show when she paraded past the front row wearing a burka. She ran backstage to cry, and when we saw her, we comforted her. She was one of the saddest creatures we'd ever met, and tragically, she took her own life in 2007.

At the Chanel show, inside the greenhouse-like space, every detail was perfect. Each chair had a seating card with the guest's full name handwritten on it in beautiful calligraphy. It really made you feel like you were there for a reason. These designers appreciated details just like we did. It might have been a different price point, but it was the same language. When the show started, on the runway there was dusty rose, gossamer-like tulle, and tweed as far as you could see. It was surreal. The models, the music, the makeup—everything worked perfectly together. Backstage, we were nervous to meet the ever-imposing Karl Lagerfeld, who was dressed in his signature black suit with stiff white collar, reed-thin after losing ninety-one pounds in thirteen months. Huddled together, we tiptoed toward him. "We've brought you a present," we said in unison. "Welcome! Welcome! I love a present," he said, putting us at ease. We handed over a black velour tracksuit with off-white monogramming that read "SLIM" and all three of us smiled for *Vogue*'s cameraman.

The Christian Lacroix show, held at L'Ecole des Beaux Arts, was one of our favorites. Lacroix is a master of color, and he painted the most romantic picture in every shade of pink with tiny peplum jackets, silk pants, and short skirts that hinted at his heyday in the 1980s. Each girl who came down the runway took your breath away. Backstage, seeing the dramatic tulle headpieces and jewels on the tables, it was confection. That show made you dream, which is what every designer wants to do. It validated for us what we had known all along: that color can be emotional and transformative, even if it's on a cotton candy–pink velour Juicy Couture tracksuit, and not a cotton candy–pink Lacroix couture dress.

The Balmain show at the Palais-Royal was a different kind of experience. It was everything people love to make fun of about fashion—Lycra bodysuits in harlequin prints, visible panty lines, and a sound track with a single line repeated over and over again, "What was I thinking? What was I thinking?" It was a shaky start for the house's then-designer Laurent Mercier, and a reminder of how tricky it is for new designers to come in and try to revive old brands while staying true to their heritage. The front-row ladies were not amused.

The East-meets-West-themed Dior show was over the top in a good way, with Chinese acrobats, kabuki makeup, and dresses in brocade, taffeta, and chiffon with ballooning volumes atop vertiginous platform shoes. The scale of the clothes was incredible. The dresses looked like parachutes floating down the runway. We had never seen clothes like that in our lives, and the spectacle! It was like a mini–Cirque du Soleil: true performance art, and fashion elevated to fantasy.

Walking backstage, we couldn't wait to meet Galliano, who looked tan and buff in white jeans and a tank top. After we said hello, he volunteered that he'd worn our track pants every day while he was designing the collection. It was really true! He was a Juicy man. Meeting him was a major moment. We were little guys and he could have spit on our shoes, but he couldn't have been more supportive. He left us with these words, which we have never forgotten: "Stay inspired." Then Daphne Guinness, the always exotically dressed British heiress and designer muse, grabbed us and said that she loved our cashmere tracksuits. We also bumped into an old friend from LA, the actress Brittany Murphy, who was at the top of her game, having just starred with Eminem in the film *8 Mile*. She had always been a Juicy fan and was wearing a black Juicy turtleneck sweater that very moment. It was a full-on Juicy pileup, and our heads were spinning.

We were still on cloud nine at the Valentino show, which was Indian-inspired, with pale pink Nehru jackets and slim satin pants. The maestro of Hollywood dressing finished with several of his signature va-va-voom-red red-carpet gowns. That night, Valentino and his partner, Giancarlo, hosted a party for us. We wore our velour pants, fur-trimmed Valentino cashmere sweaters, and Juicy T-shirts. As gifts, we brought Valentino a red velour tracksuit monogrammed with "VaVa" and other styles for Giancarlo and Valentino's handsome Brazilian head of PR, Carlos Souza, who was instrumental in organizing the event.

Arriving at Giancarlo's penthouse atop a 1930s building on the Left Bank's Quai d'Orsay was another pinch-me moment. With a view of the Seine, the apartment was actually a combination of three residences, crafted by fashion-world architect Peter Marino. Inside, the architecture was contemporary-looking and spare, but the décor was eclectic and the art to die for.

The way Giancarlo incorporated modern art into his living space was unlike anything we'd ever seen. Our mouths fell open when we saw two Andy Warhol Lenins, one red and one black, on a wall in the dining room, and a Cy Twombly over the marble fireplace in the living room. A Francis Bacon painting was hanging in front of the bay window overlooking the river, the curving lines on the canvas echoing the curves of the window. And there was a Rothko we couldn't take our eyes off of. The furniture was a mix of gorgeous antiques by the likes of Jean-Michel Frank, Eileen

Gray, and Jacques Adnet, in addition to a seventeenth-century Japanese lacquer chest. There is luxury and then there is this. It was a taste level we'd never experienced.

The way he entertained was enviable, too. Dinner was served buffet style (silver platters overflowing with squid-ink pasta and risotto) so everyone could mingle. And we felt so welcome. It was the first time we'd met British journalists Sarah Mower and Alexandra Shulman, and the legendary *International Herald Tribune* fashion editor Suzy Menkes, who said she was a fan because we brought color and fun back to fashion. Everyone at the party wanted to know about our volume. They couldn't believe we had made more than one million tracksuits. We were the biggest brand at many American department stores at the time, outselling the likes of Tommy Hilfiger and Ralph Lauren. It was such a foreign concept to them.

That evening was everything we liked in a party and still do. It wasn't formal, but it was beautiful, like the most superchic family dinner you've ever been to. It was the beginning of a long friendship with Giancarlo, built on our respect for his incredible partnership with Valentino. Spending that much time with a business partner is rare, which is something we have in common with them. They were kids when they started building their empire fifty-plus years ago, and they stuck together. That's unusual. Most partnerships break up. But Giancarlo and Valentino still go everywhere together, just like us.

Being in Paris, of course we took time out to shop. The

first stop was Hermès on Rue de Faubourg. Pam wanted a pair of buttery-soft leather gloves, but only if they were cropped. Hermès didn't have any fingerless gloves, but that didn't stop her. Pam asked the saleswoman for a pair of scissors and chopped off the fingers in front of her. We also bought collars for our dogs Tink and Dan, Bob, and Sid Vicious. A few months later, poor Bob was eaten by an owl and buried in a Hermès box, but we digress.

At Didier Ludot, Paris's premiere vintage store at the Palais-Royal, we couldn't quite reconcile spending $6,000 on an Yves Saint Laurent coat from the 1970s. To us, vintage was about the thrill of the hunt and getting a deal. We had more fun at the Left Bank resale stores, where Pam bought a Patou cloche hat, and Gela a cropped white fox-fur coat. We also went to the flea market known as Les Puces de Saint-Ouen, the largest antiques market in the world. It was the mother lode of amazing stuff priced well. It was a visual feast looking at all the vintage clothes, Chanel costume jewelry, and furniture. This was our kind of stomping ground. Pam bought two chandeliers and had them shipped home. That day was the beginning of a long friendship with Hamish Bowles, who was our tour guide. Hamish has a crazy knowledge and passion about couture. Being with him is like being with a walking fashion dictionary. He's the Cecil Beaton of our generation.

Another day, we went to Frédéric Malle to see how fragrance was made. We went into glass humidor-like rooms to smell individual essences and it turned out we liked all the same notes. We loved the essence of tuberose. It was flowery but not overly so. That day was a great education about notes, layers, and dry down. That's where we fell in love with the Frédéric Malle scent Carnal Flower, which inspired our first Juicy fragrance.

We also stopped into a vintage jewelry store. It was raining and the store was closing, but we banged on the door and got them to let us in. We each wanted to buy a piece to commemorate the trip, something major that was a reminder to not to forget the magic. Pam bought a Georgian-era diamond tremblant flower pin, and Gela an Art Deco diamond-and-pearl ring. By then, we were over our limits on our AmEx cards, and had to call our finance person and say, "Put it through!"

As a final treat, on our last night we booked ourselves into the famous Ritz Hotel, built in 1898 by Hardouin-Mansart, who also designed the Palace of Versailles. Overlooking Place Vendôme, the hotel has hosted practically every royal, head of state, and celebrity in the world, including Ernest Hemingway, Elton John, and Princess Diana. We were ready to party, LA style. So we put on our best Chanel suits and crocodile Manolos and headed to the dining room. We had a champagne-soaked dinner, with hours spent devouring the waiters' stories about when the Nazis occupied the hotel during World War II. We had many courses, starting with caviar and ending with crème brûlée, and all the bread and butter we could stuff in our mouths.

Then we put on our bathing suits and went for a late-night dip in the famous Ritz indoor pool, which is inspired by ancient Greek and Roman baths. Dripping wet, with champagne glasses still in hand, we decided we had to see Coco Chanel's suite, where she lived for thirty-five years beginning in the 1920s. We roamed the halls in our Ritz bathrobes going from room to room knocking on doors. We eventually found the suite, but not before hotel security found us. Somehow, we convinced them to give us a peek. Inside, much of the décor is as she left it, including the baroque mirrors, rock crystals on the tables, and red lacquered Coromandel screens. Again, it was like a dream.

The next morning at the airport, we were wiped out. We had so much luggage because of all of our shopping, that the airline representatives kept weighing it and weighing it and weighing it. We had to pay extra to get on the plane with it all. We also had two enormous boxes of Ladurée macarons to keep up with, which we had bought for our new partners Paul Charron and Angela Ahrendts at Liz Claiborne. We were flying directly to New York to see them and meet one hundred of the top Liz Claiborne executives for the first time. It was our first ever corporate board meeting and we had no idea what to expect. Once again, we were leaving one world and diving into a totally new one.

Being in that scene at the Paris haute couture, we had arrived. That everyone knew who we were was an eye-opener. We were changing fashion and they knew it. In its post–World War II heyday, haute couture was its own kind of lifestyle dressing, with wealthy women from all over the world coming to Paris every season to order their wardrobes. It was for a time when you changed your clothes to go to lunch and wore white tie for dinner. What we were doing was lifestyle dressing for a different time. And seeing the collections in Paris only made us stronger in our conviction to dress the world. The haute couture may have been losing ground to casual luxury brands like Juicy Couture, but at that shining moment, there was still room for both. It was high and low at its finest.

Chapter 10
The Juicy-Corporate Mind Meld

When we pulled up to the Liz Claiborne headquarters at 1441 Broadway, in the heart of New York's garment district, we had no idea what kind of transition was ahead with the Juicy-corporate mind meld. We were dressed in our Juicy version of corporate attire: matching camel corduroy miniskirts and blazers, "Smells like Couture" striped tube socks, and "Choose Juicy" T-shirts. And we'd managed to salvage the few Ladurée macarons we hadn't demolished on our flight from Paris to New York and consolidate them into one box to present as a gift to our new bosses, Liz Claiborne Chief Executive Officer Paul Charron and Executive Vice President Angela Ahrendts.

When we arrived at Paul's office, he had a gift for us, too. He knew we liked candy, and that it was part of our Juicy culture, so his wife had made up a special candy bowl for us with Jolly Ranchers, Hersey's Kisses, and more. And when we saw it, we instantly felt welcome. We shook hands, sat down, and settled in to listen to Paul lay out the values of the Liz Claiborne brand. "We're a humble family," he said, "based on traditional values." We nodded our heads enthusiastically, all the while slouching down in our seats and trying to forget our Paris shopping insanity, Ritz Hotel escapades, and frantic calls to up our AmEx limits. Paul explained what was on tap for our first day—a meeting with the top one hundred executives at the company, including the presidents of the thirty other Liz Claiborne divisions. They wanted to know about their latest Juicy acquisition. It was a dog and pony show, and we were the star attraction.

After we were prepped, he took us upstairs and threw open the doors to the corporate auditorium. There they were, our new colleagues: a sea of gray suits. And here we came, two LA crazies in camel corduroy miniskirts and "Smells like Couture" tube socks trotting down the aisle to the stage.

They seemed excited and delighted to see us, clapping and cheering when we introduced ourselves. We proceeded to lead one of our "Viva La Juicy" pep rallies. "We have incredible Juicy dreams," we said. "We want to dress the world! If we can do it, anyone can!" The suits went wild.

The Liz Claiborne team had prepared a PowerPoint

presentation that charted the growth of our company, and showed where they wanted to take Juicy by giving us money and systems to open company-owned retail stores, adding more international distribution, licensing product extensions, and launching a fragrance. We had never seen a PowerPoint presentation. When we looked out into the audience, we knew what they were seeing: dollar signs on a pink slot machine. "Bling, bling, bling!"

After our speech, we took some questions. One woman raised her hand and asked us to name our favorite "moderate designer." We said, "What's 'moderate'?" We didn't realize she was using the term "moderate," meaning brands that sell sportswear and career wear in the $100 range, like Liz Claiborne and, they thought, Juicy Couture. We'd never heard that term, which amused the suits even more. Laughter ensued. It was up there with the "IT platform" and "shrinkage" moment from our first meeting with the Clairbornians in LA. We had entered a new world and we needed to learn a whole new language.

We stuck around for two days of meetings in the offices, during which we felt like the most popular girls in school. All the division presidents were calling on us with ideas about how they could tap into our business and make money for the corporation. There were so many possibilities, they told us, and the sky was the limit. We knew we had something great with Juicy, and we wanted to spread it around, but it was a lot to take in at the beginning.

Some of the people who came at us had great ideas. Ed

Bucciarelli, the head of accessories, understood immediately that Juicy could translate into a full line of bags and jewelry. And Art Spiro, the head of fragrance, was ready to give us the blueprint we needed to launch a perfume, and let us do the creative part.

Other people brought ideas that didn't seem like the right fit. One of them was for a licensed line of Juicy raincoats. We thought, Juicy raincoats? We're SoCal girls; we don't even know what rain is. Then there was an idea for a line of Juicy Lanz nightgowns. We said, "Lanz nightgowns? The frilly ones from Salzburg that you wear on Christmas morning? Pam's Pilgrim grandmother from Rhode Island was into those." We loved them when we were kids, but not *now.* "But this license could be ten million dollars a year, and that one could be thirty million, and you'll get a percentage," they said, trying to entice us. After we heard "Lanz nightgowns," it was all white noise. It wouldn't have mattered if they'd said we could make a trillion dollars. We could not be bought.

We were aware of the pitfalls of licensing the wrong way, having read all about Calvin Klein suing Warnaco, the manufacturer and distributor of Calvin Klein underwear and jeans, for diluting his brand name with unauthorized sales to discount stores such as Costco and Sam's Club. (They reached a settlement right before the case went to trial.) And at the end of the day, even though we had a deal with an earn out that was sales-driven, we didn't want to whore out our brand. It wasn't about selling the shit out of it and then getting out. We wanted to keep it Juicy. And for us, Juicy was forever.

You have to look at licensing and what it does to your brand and how it moves it up in the world. We worked hard to hold the line and choose what worked for us, not what was brand-inappropriate—like licensing raincoats. Licensing raincoats was a really missy, or rather "moderate," way of thinking. But it wasn't a Juicy way of thinking. Juicy was a contemporary brand, and there was no such thing as a coat department on the contemporary floor of a department store.

You are the keeper of the brand; that's what a founder is. And if you don't keep it pure and authentic, you're done. That's the main point of choosing the right financial partner, whether you sell to them outright or they are buying into your business for equity. You want someone who lets you be the keeper of the brand and make key strategic decisions. Because once it shifts and your partner has different ideas, it's over. O-V-E-R, over.

We moved forward on some things, licensing accessories and fragrance in-house at Liz Claiborne. After that, our first outside license was with Movado to develop Juicy Couture watches. And there were many, many more licenses after that.

After a couple of seriously surreal days, we headed home to LA. It was hard to believe that news of the sale of Juicy to Liz Claiborne hadn't even been announced to the public yet. But the day was coming, and Angela was traveling to Pacoima so she could be with us when she broke the news, and help us tell our staff.

On the day the sale was announced, March 18, 2003, we did feel like we had won the lottery. We made it! We had gone from the Paris haute couture to the executive offices of Liz Claiborne, and we'd made a chunk of change on a business we started with $200, a business where the first salary we took was $27,000 a year. Now we were millionaires. We were the American Dream and we were girls. We weren't Harvard grads, and we weren't MBAs. We were two best friends who beat the odds and did it our way, in LA, laughing and schlemiel schlimazel–ing our way through every step.

But we also felt like we had been to war. We did it: We made the money. But we were petrified.

Angela sat down at one of our desks, picked up the handset of one of our filthy phones, and started calling all our retailers one after another—Bloomingdale's, Saks Fifth Avenue, Neiman Marcus, Fred Segal—telling them all that Liz Claiborne had bought Juicy Couture but that everything was going to stay exactly the same. Her message was "business as usual." But listening to her, we knew that wasn't true.

At some point in the entrepreneurial story arc, if you build a successful business, there will come a time when you have to make some tough adult decisions that are emotionally painful but are the best thing for the brand. And we knew that time was upon us. That's why we were cowering in the bathroom hugging each other, with tears streaming down our faces. We thought, What have we done? It felt like we were about to get a blood transfusion, that they were going to drain out all the old and fill it up with the new.

We invited all two hundred members of our staff into the warehouse. Angela called it a "town hall meeting," which was a term we'd never heard before. We introduced her and told them we'd sold the business and not to worry. And there they all were, Janey, Vicki, Elva, and the rest of our Juicy family, looking at us wide-eyed, like "Mom and Dad, what is up?" Of course, they had known something was up, because we'd always had an open-door policy in our office, and for the last few months, we were constantly telling people to get out. Then there had been all the weird suits in the warehouse. But it was still a surprise, and they were apprehensive.

Then it was Angela's turn to lead the pep rally on behalf of Liz Claiborne, the new parent. She told our employees, "We are here to reassure, not to frighten. We don't want to change your culture. We want you to stay Juicy. We think you are amazing! We love your product. We're here to help you make your dreams come true, and turn this into the next great American brand."

But we knew the reality was that the finance and warehouse departments were going to go to Liz Claiborne, and some of our people were going to lose their jobs. After the meeting, we just kept boohooing and asking Angela, "Who is going to go?" Our finance department had been involved in the whole negotiation leading up to the sale, so those people were aware that they weren't going to have jobs under the new regime. The prospect of losing the people in our warehouse was harder, especially Elva, our first employee. They were the ones who'd won the washers and dryers during the Halloween pageants, and who'd made the enchiladas for the Christmas parties. They helped us build the business and had tremendous pride in Juicy. That very day we came up with a list of people whose jobs we wanted to save. We called it our get-out-of-jail-free list. And Elva's name was on it.

The first order of business in the first few days after the sale was announced was to move our warehouse operations to the Liz Claiborne warehouse in Santa Fe Springs. What we didn't realize was how fast and big a machine Liz Claiborne was, and what it was going to feel like to have our office infiltrated by teams of their people making decisions about who at Juicy was going to stay and who was going to go. They were going through everything, looking at our IT, our office space, and our warehouse and deciding which processes had to change, which caused a lot of resistance. It was chaos. Nobody knew who they should be answering to, and every five minutes someone would burst through our door, freaking out about the new way things had to be done.

The manager of the Liz Claiborne warehouse was looking at all our employees to see if their skills would translate to the Santa Fe Springs facility. He wasn't finding a lot of people who made the cut from abacus to computer, and our people were starting to fall apart from the pressure. So Gela went to nail him against the wall, and tell him what was what. But that's not exactly what went down. She blurted out a few choice words. Then he looked at her and put it to her straight: "You are now part of a corporation, and you work for the good of that corporation, just like me. I work for the retirement accounts and the well-being of every person at Liz Claiborne, and the stockholders who believe in the dream of Liz Claiborne. I have to look at the stock value, and that means I have to look at the shipping. And your people are not capable of dealing with the complex, computerized systems required to ship a business that is growing at the rate you're growing. So the stock is eventually going to plummet and it's going to hurt me and you and it's going to hurt the whole corporation. You're part of a new family now."

It was a rude awakening. We realized a corporation views things differently than an entrepreneurial company does. A corporation is looking at the whole, while we were just looking at Juicy, our people, our personalities, and our emotions. In the end, the new warehouse manager didn't want Elva to move to Santa Fe Springs. So we had to find a new position for her in our office. It was necessary growth, and once we understood the changes, and why they were right for the brand, we were all for them. Liz Claiborne's managers weren't being mean, there was just a bigger picture out there, and different people to look after. And it was our job to be supportive of our new colleagues at Liz Claiborne and help the transition go smoothly.

Luckily, the sense we had about Paul and Angela from the beginning was bearing itself out. Although we were merging two very different worlds, we were respectful of each other. In Angela, we had the most amazing mentor to help us navigate the maze of unknowns. She was the reason the transition worked so well, and Paul came to understand who we were and what was so amazing about Juicy. She respected our alien culture and allowed it to live and grow. And she knew how to finesse the art and commerce sides of a business and make them work together. Most suits don't know how to do that. She taught us how to communicate with Paul, and Paul how to communicate with us. If something happened and we freaked out, she would tell us how to weigh the pros and cons, and present them to Paul, which usually involved trading e-mails back and forth in our trademark, fairy tale–like Fluffian speak. (We had taken to calling ourselves Fluffy and Fluffy, so he called us Fluffians. We called him Sugar Daddy because he held the purse strings.)

One of the things Paul was always trying to do in his role as CEO was to create synergy between the brands in the Liz Claiborne portfolio. And he thought Juicy could have synergy with European fast-fashion brand Mexx, which had been brought into the Liz fold in 2001. He wanted us to leave our beautiful, high-end showroom in Antwerp, which handled our sales in the Benelux countries, where Juicy was shown alongside such prestigious designer brands as Chloé and Stella McCartney, and move into the Mexx Antwerp showroom. It might not sound like a big deal. A showroom is a showroom, right? Well, no.

This wasn't a good move for Juicy and we knew it. We told Angela we didn't want to go along with Paul's suggestion, and she suggested that we do some research and show him some evidence to justify why he should foot the bill for Juicy to be in a fancy showroom in Antwerp when it could be in the Mexx showroom, which Liz Claiborne owned, for free. So we hit the Internet and started looking. We needed to find a way to articulate what we knew about our brand and needed him to know. We found an article about Ralph Lauren and why he'd spent $20 million to open a massive, twenty-four-thousand-square-foot, four-story flagship at #1 New Bond Street in London in 1998, when he already had a smaller store up the road. His answer was simple: "Image, stupid."

We brought the article to Paul and read it to him. When we got to the words, "Image, stupid," you could have heard a pin drop in the room. It was dead silence and we were shaking. We thought he was going to storm out. But he understood our point. Juicy was an image-based business. It might have been casual luxury, but it was the crème de la crème. And we had to preserve that aura of wantability in every way we could, even down to the look of the showroom where the line was presented. Image is not what Liz Claiborne's moderate brands were about. But it was what we were about. Juicy couldn't move into the Mexx showroom, and it didn't. We were learning from them, but they were also learning from us. Juicy was the first out-of-the-box contemporary brand that Liz Claiborne added to their stable. They owned the moderate, bridge, department-store world, and didn't understand that our brand was about prestige and hype and celebrity product placement. It was a new game. For us during that time, the secret to survival was to "Say what you mean, mean what you say, and don't say it mean."

Another change we knew was coming was that we had to move some of our production from Los Angeles to the factories that Liz Claiborne owned in Hong Kong. We had a hard time with that one. "Made in the Glamorous U.S.A." had always been a part of the Juicy story. It was real and authentic and people appreciated it. And Los Angeles was our home. Not to mention the amount of money and manufacturing we brought to the city, and the doors we opened to anyone who wanted to start a T-shirt or knitwear line in Los Angeles. We were afraid to make things on the other side of the world, where we couldn't touch them or try them on. But that was part of the deal.

As difficult as some aspects of the transition were, there were some perks—like having funds to shoot our first Juicy campaign, not that we had any idea how to approach it. Angela gave us money, and being the kind of girls we are, we picked up the phone and called Ellen von Unwerth ourselves. It didn't even faze us. Ellen was one of the most famous female fashion photographers; she had shot a lot of our favorite ad campaigns, and her work had a girl-power spirit. God knows how we got her number, but we did. And she was very nice, but a bit confused.

She asked, "Who's producing the shoot?" And we said, "We are!" She said, "Who's your location scout?" And we said, "We are!" We didn't know that it was common practice to hire an advertising agency to coordinate a team for a fashion shoot, or that we needed to get permits from the city to shoot! We were do-it-yourselfers, and just thought we could kamikaze it. We gave Ellen the dates, decided on a fee, and that was that. The Danish blonde model we hired was a family friend, May Andersen (who was then Stephen Dorff's girlfriend), the stylist was an LA girl we'd known forever named Arianne Phillips (who works with Madonna and is now an Oscar-nominated costume designer), and the locations we used were all our favorite local spots, including the seafood shack/biker hangout Neptune's Net on the Pacific Coast Highway. We didn't make it a big thing; we just ordered French fries and started shooting. They didn't let us shoot inside, so we just stole shots outside. We did the whole thing over one crazy day.

The clothes were a mix of Juicy and our collection of vintage. The model was wearing double braids, a rainbow logo tee, a pompom hat, and Juicy track pants. It was total SoCal punk-rock luxury. In the end, the photos were gorgeous and so Juicy. There was something so gratifying about being able to take all of our creative inspirations and dreams and bring them to life on a bigger scale. It was like, Hello! We're here, like it or not!

But it's a miracle it worked out in the end. We didn't plan room for text on the images, and we didn't know to tell Ellen to format the photos to fit a billboard. By the time it was all said and done, we had to collage together three photos to fit the billboard space we rented on Sunset Boulevard near the Chateau Marmont. And any time we interviewed an ad agency after that, we always asked the team, "Can you do a picture to fit a billboard?" As if anyone would have that problem but us.

Angela also gave us carte blanche to redecorate our offices. She said, "Anything your heart desires. Make it your dream!" Well, we've always been good at decorating our own homes, but we didn't know we could have hired anyone to decorate our offices. Instead, we hired a guy who worked around the corner from us in Pacoima. He was a contractor, not a decorator.

He put in a light beige carpet, which our first mistake, because we were going through a pomegranate phase at the time. Every day, we'd eat at least two whole pomegranates each, ripping them apart like wild animals at our desks. It looked like there was a murder in our design studio! The Clairbornians brought in legit office chairs, which might have been ergonomically correct but looked like something out of a science-fiction film. The main feature we told the contractor we needed in our design space was a platform, because whenever we were sitting down, doing fittings, we could never see the model's bottom half.

He didn't really install a platform; it was more of a ledge that was four feet off the ground with poles on either side. They looked like stripper poles! And Juicy turned into Nudes, Nudes, Nudes!

When Angela came to visit next, she couldn't wait to see our new design space. She walked in and gasped, gulped, and because she was relentlessly supportive, said, "It's great!"

We knew it was horrible, but we weren't going to do it again. Spending a lot of money on our offices was not in our nature. We still were thinking frugally, at least when it came to those kinds of things. Besides, we knew we weren't going to get any inspiration there, because it didn't come from a room. We were more comfortable holding our inner sanctum staff meetings where we always had, in the bathroom! The pink tile, high school–looking bathroom was also our de facto gym, with an elliptical trainer and treadmill that never got any use; nap corner with cheapo massage chair; goodie closet full of Juicy clothes and handbags that were doled out generously to anyone who deserved snaps; and makeup and hair staging area cluttered with pink wigs, false eyelashes, lipstick, and anything else you might need for an impromptu night out (or Halloween costume).

But it was in the new design studio with the stripper poles that we met for our first quarterly earnings review in

June. Paul instituted a policy of having quarterly reviews, which was really kind of brilliant, because it kept us in check with the suits and the suits in check with us.

We gathered around the table with Paul and Angela, all the key people from our side and theirs. If it sounds like a showdown, it was—Juicy calling Liz on the pomegranate crime-scene carpet. We had a serious problem. For all their talk about their newfangled, state-of-the-art warehouse, we were down $14 million in shipping. In other words, we were behind shipping $14 million worth of Juicy merchandise to stores, and our customers were screaming for their product. It was mostly our small stores, too, which were the boutiques that had been with us since the beginning, because Liz Claiborne was a department store–based business, and the warehouse was not used to shipping small orders.

The transition to a new warehouse and a new finance system had taken in toll. We were furious, especially since a lot of people in our warehouse had been let go. We might have had archaic ways of doing things, with homemade formulas, but we had never fallen behind shipping $14 million in orders before the Claibornians waltzed into Pacoima. And at that point we really wondered, "What have we done?" Maybe selling our company was a mistake.

But that's when we really saw the power of Liz Claiborne. Angela said, "Don't worry. We've dealt with this before and we can do it again."

This powerful corporation with a mega-infrastructure and a lot of people who wanted to help us succeed rallied around us. And we realized then that we could stomp our feet and say, "There's a huge problem!" and someone would be there trying to solve it. We weren't alone anymore.

We know now that it was inevitable we were going to fall behind because of the transition. Businesses are fast-moving machines. And there was going to be a dip before there was a surge.

By the next quarter, the meeting was a love fest. Instead of a showdown, we shared our earnings with the Clabornians in a song. Yes, we sang our earnings report. We had a nickname for our Direct Operating Profit. We called it the DOPE. And we gave them a lot of DOPE. It was only just beginning.

Surviving the Transition to Corporate Management

A corporation views things differently than an entrepreneurial company does. Everything is for the good of the whole.

You're part of a new family now. Learn to speak their language, but teach them some of yours, too.

You will have to make some adult decisions about the best thing for the brand, and that may involve restructuring your staff.

Don't be seduced by dollar signs. Only license if it moves your brand up in the world.

There may be a dip before there is a surge. In other words, you may fall behind on production during the transition, but you will recover.

Don't be afraid to say no if you can explain your rationale. You are the keeper of the brand. If you don't keep it pure and authentic, you're done.

Chapter 11

Hands-on Branding

Together with Liz Claiborne, we were ready to transform Juicy Couture from an LA-based casual luxury line to a global fashion brand. It was going to be a culmination of everything we'd done before, from creating our own homemade Rue de Branford Juicy Couture notepads, to actually producing a full line of Juicy Couture school supplies and gift items for real. Once the crack in the door had been opened, we were ready to put our stamp on everything. We wanted to rule the world, remember?

Well, ruling the world wasn't as easy as we thought. In the first few months after we sold, we didn't kick back and take long lunches at Pacoima's finest establishment, Big

Jim's, after all. We were working harder than ever juggling media requests, meeting with licensees, and reviewing everything from an offer from Mattel to make a Juicy Couture Barbie (hell, yeah!), to an offer from a production company to star in our own reality TV show (not then, not now, and not ever). We did accept an invitation to be on *The Oprah Winfrey Show*, where we appeared in matching tube socks, striped scarves, miniskirts, and jean jackets. That was a new high.

It was an intensely creative period, during which we were working on a lot of projects simultaneously: licensing accessories and swimwear, opening our own Juicy Couture branded stores, and launching our first fragrance. And we were doing it all while designing Juicy Couture's six women's, six children's, and four men's collections that came out each year.

We'd come a long way from sewing the elastic bands on maternity jeans and writing a thank-you note to include with every shipment. But we were still very hands-on because we still believed, even though our business was big, it had to be personal.

When big companies license new product categories, they often staff up with specialized designers to work on those projects. While we did have the in-house teams at Liz Claiborne working on our jewelry and bags, we didn't have dedicated designers working on swimwear, shoes, and other categories. We had us. Why? For one, we were having the time of our lives. We wanted to do it all, from shopping for antique glassware to inspire our perfume bottle, to inspecting the charms for our charm bracelets to make sure they had real moving parts, to obsessing over what we would look like as Pam and Gela Barbie dolls. (Our sample sewers had a field day with that one, coming up with all kinds of mini–Juicy outfits. In the end, we wore pink and green terry outfits and had our dogs Tink and Bob in the box with us, in collars with tiny J-pulls.)

Another reason we were so hands-on is that we felt strongly about maintaining control. When you're setting up any kind of license, you better be all over it, with eyes on the product and an appreciation for the fine details and keeping the look aspirational. Because the minute it gets away from you there's going to be trouble.

For two girls who love the beach, swimwear was a no-brainer. We signed a license with Swim Anywhere, one of the largest swimwear manufacturers in the country, which had an office in Manhattan Beach. The design process was a dream. When we went down to meet with the founder, Rosemarie di Lorenzo, she decorated the studio in Juicy colors, put out lots of candy, and even served cocktails with umbrellas in them. We wanted to bring our fun, colorful sensibility to the water, which meant reversible hot-pink and kelly-green suits in Lycra and terry cloth, emblazoned with the Juicy crest and "Love G&P." They were designed to be mixed and matched, just like our tracksuits, and included low-rise, side-tie, and boy-short bottoms that could be paired with cap-sleeve crop tops, bandeaus, or triangle tops. Some of the pieces were embellished with ruffles, chain belts, or charms, which were all things we liked, and things that were becoming Juicy design signatures that carried over into other product categories.

We thought it would be fun to host a runway show and star-studded garden party in Los Angeles to launch Juicy Beach. We planned the event for July 31, 2004. Our publicist, Lara Shriftman, had the invitations printed on pink-and-green kickboards, and the venue was the Burndorf Estate. (You may remember it from the 1981 film *Mommie Dearest.*) The 1939 home, with a huge expanse of green backyard and crystal-blue swimming pool, is so Beverly Hills ladylike and beautiful. Everything was done in a color palette of pink and green, which was our way of spoofing and giving a nod to the preppy country-club scene we loved so much. We served gimlets and petit fours with "G&P" written on the tops in icing. And everyone came, including tennis superstar sisters Venus and Serena Williams, Owen and Luke Wilson, Fergie, Kate Beckinsale, Nicole Richie, Selma Blair, Courteney Cox and David Arquette, Farrah Fawcett, even Penny Marshall. Lara Flynn Boyle wore one of our "Juicy Loves Martha" tank tops. (Martha Stewart had just been jailed and we were devastated.) And our lucky charm Sandra Bernhard was our MC at the fashion show. People had such a good time they didn't want to leave, even after it got dark. It was the perfect LA fashion party.

We launched accessories around the same time, too, but with less fanfare. We had been working on the line with

Ed Bucciarelli, Liz Claiborne's Group president of accessories, and his team, who came out from New York every few weeks. Before they came out the first time, we went vintaging for inspiration, just like we always do. We hit Shareen in downtown LA, Golyester on La Brea, and Palace Costume in Hollywood. We found tons of bags from the 1960s and '70s, including some granny doctor-bag styles. Ed's team built an infrastructure with a SKU plan and guided us through the process of making sure we had a variety of sizes, from midsize to totes, wallets, and, in our case, dog carriers.

We worked with their design team to come up with the right shapes, leathers, and trims. We wanted to make a big statement with color and charms and bring casual fabrications like terry and velour to accessories. We also wanted to bring the whimsy of our world to the category. What was on the inside had to be just as fun as what was on the outside. You'd open a bag and there would be a mirror emblazoned with the word "Look" and a pocket emblazoned with a "$" for your money. One of our biggest hits was the Daydreamer, a tote bag with drawstring top that featured a silk ribbon tied in a bow. It was a bestseller for years, and everyone copied it.

Our accessories launch was so successful that we were honored at the Accessories Council Excellence Awards in November 2005 in New York for best new launch of the year, alongside fashion heavyweights Tom Ford and Sean "P. Diddy" Combs. As always, our old pal Sandra Bernhard was there to present the award to us, "Two women who certainly know—and live by—the mantra that one can never be without too many accessories."

At the same time, we were also meeting with the jewelry team. The first designer Liz Claiborne sent us was not a good fit. Her jewelry was so bad, it looked like it came out of a gumball machine. She went back to New York and told our bosses we were bitches. But we stood our ground. We wanted quality. We wanted Arnold Ephraums, who had worked for Christian Dior, Balenciaga, and Guess. He understood our taste level. We had always loved charms, ever since our mothers gave us charm bracelets when we were teens, which kicked off a lifelong passion of adding charms to them. That's what we thought should be the starting point for our accessories collection. So our first piece was a charm bracelet, and the charms Arnold made blew us away. He made birds in birdcages that had a button you could push to make the bird move around, slot machines with moving arms, diamond-ring charms, mini–logo tee charms, anything that was iconically Juicy. We also made chunky statement necklaces, hoop earrings, and bracelets designed to be layered.

Opening stores was also a top priority in our strategy for growth. A store is your home, your opportunity to merchandise your brand and show the world how you see it, not how the buyer at another store sees it. It's your vision from storefront to shopping bag, your living billboard with your DNA all over it.

The location for our first store was going to be Las Vegas, inside Caesars Forum Shops. Las Vegas wasn't a fashion center like LA or New York, but it was the crossroads of the world, with the equivalent of the entire population of the city turning over every seven to ten days. Caesars Forum is one of the most heavily trafficked malls in the country. And we'd seen the success that the owners of Lucky Brand (also in the Liz Claiborne family) had with their store there, so we went for it. And we printed money in that store, even if it wasn't everything we dreamed of aesthetically.

Angela told us to find the architect of our dreams and visit stores that we loved to take note of our favorite design details. We really liked the dressing rooms in Stella McCartney's Meatpacking District boutique in New York City, which we thought had elements that could be incorporated into a full-blown store format for Juicy. They felt personal, not cold like so many retail spaces. They were what we imagined it would be like walking into Stella's bedroom, with beautiful lacquered fixtures and floral wallpaper with postcards, necklaces, and other knickknacks pinned to the walls.

We hired the London-based design firm Universal, which had worked on that store. And they turned out to be the most un-Juicy guys ever. They didn't get our pink world, our soft edges, or our girlishness. We told them we wanted a beautiful inlaid wood floor in a herringbone pattern. They were into concrete, not "timber," as they called it. They stuck up their British noses at "timber." That should have been a sign. We should have jumped out of the way of their swinging logs. We weren't speaking the same language. And we found out, although they did design Stella's store, they didn't do the dressing rooms!

The whole experience was difficult. We won some and they won some. We kept referencing Fiorucci, a store we'd loved since childhood. They understood that, thank God, and that we wanted a modular look so we could change props often and make things look fresh in the store. But in the end, the heavy metal fixtures and streamlined modern lounge look did not reflect our vision. They took our humor and put it in the floor, which had our slogan "Dude, Where's My Couture?" spelled out in cold, dark granite.

Luckily, we had a great visual merchandiser to save the day. Humberto Leon, who since founded the supercool chain of stores called Opening Ceremony with his partner, Carol Lim, and is designing the Kenzo label, made the space palatable. He filled the windows with candy and colored sand, and the vitrines with charms, jewelry, and other cool enough stuff to give the store an edge.

To open the store on November 20, 2004, we threw one of our best parties yet, beginning with the four hot-pink Juicy jets we chartered to fly our guests from LA to Las Vegas. We even had a hot-pink carpet leading up to the jets on the tarmac at the Burbank Airport, and the flight attendants were decked out in Juicy Couture, naturally.

Sin City didn't know what hit it when Juicy touched

down. Pamela Anderson, Courtney Love, Nicky Hilton, Rebecca Romijn and Jerry O'Connell, Anthony Kiedis, John Cusack, and many more celebs came out to party with us, starting at the boutique, where they sipped champagne and nibbled G&P chocolates. The after-party was at a new burlesque club called Forty Deuce. For the final striptease of the evening, dancers were clad in Juicy jeans and fur coats. But not for long!

It was a great party because Liz Claiborne gave us a budget and let us be us. Even if the next day, a freak snowstorm made the trip back to LA in the Juicy jets a bit harrowing, especially after so much bubbly. After we landed, Courtney Love said, "That flight was the scariest thing that ever happened to me." And that's saying something.

Developing our first fragrance was another major undertaking. We'd already been to Paris and met the famous nose Frédéric Malle, who'd educated us about notes and dry down. So when we met with the team from Firmenich, the Swiss company that created the Juicy juice, we had ideas about what it should smell like. We wanted to start with notes that smelled like the real essence of a rare white flower. We wanted something that smelled clean, not like chemicals, which was a hard thing to do with a commercial fragrance. Again, we wanted to elevate and not do something that smelled like candy. It had to smell like couture.

When it came to the bottle, the fragrance team was trying to push us in the direction of what was popular then, which was Thierry Mugler's Angel, bottled in a sculptural star. But that wasn't us. You don't win following others, you win when you have a new idea. We wanted a bottle based on an antique alcohol decanter we'd found at Guinevere Antiques on Kings Road in London. It was a beautiful crystal bottle with a chain and padlock around the neck, which, as the story went, was there to keep servants out of the liquor cabinet. We liked the idea of a having an accessory attached to our perfume bottle, a little something extra that could be worn as a necklace. (It's all about the details.)

We had ideas about packaging, too—we wanted a clean, elegant box with heavy paper stock, something elevated in feeling, like the Ladurée macaron boxes we'd fallen in love with in Paris, but in the pink-and-brown color combination we designated for our Juicy packaging. We wanted the box to resemble a vanity, with a mirrored backdrop, a top that flips down to reveal the contents, and a tiny pullout drawer with a diary inside. It was as much about how the fragrance would look in your house as how it smelled.

In the end, every detail was gorgeous, from our fairy tale printed in script on the inside of the box, to the silver metal crest with our dogs and "Love G&P" on the bottle, to the tiny crowns on the end of the drawer pull on the box. The necklace was a locket with a functioning lock and key. It was more expensive packaging than Liz Claiborne's in-house fragrance team was used to doing, and we had to push them a little bit. But it was worth it. Everything about our fragrance looked expensive, and we were really proud of the result. Now everyone has whimsical perfume bottles. Look at Vera Wang's Princess fragrance with the jeweled crown cap, and Marc Jacobs's Daisy, with the pop-art flowers on the cap. We ushered in a new era of whimsical fragrance bottles as decorative accessories.

To launch our fragrance and help take the brand to the next level, we needed a creative shop that would work with us to come up with a brand message that would be consistent across all the product categories. That's where an advertising agency comes in, we learned. Before Liz Claiborne, Angela had been the president of Donna Karan for six years, where she witnessed the incredible partnership between Donna and her brand guru Trey Laird, who was corporate creative director of Donna Karan from 1993 to 2002. Together with Peter Arnell, Trey created the iconic campaign for DKNY, Karan's younger, more accessible casual brand that launched in 1989. The images of the New York skyline, the colors, speed, and patterns of the city that never sleeps were on every bus, bus stop, and billboard. They became synonymous with New York City, 1990s fashion, and, of course, DKNY. Those images brought Donna enormous success. So Angela told us to go out and find our Trey Laird.

In LA, there weren't any big fashion ad agencies. So we got a list of four of the top agencies in New York and went to look at their books. As it happened, Trey Laird had recently left Donna Karan to form his own agency, Laird+Partners, and our last meeting was with him. Trey was a charming guy, had a daughter who was obsessed with Juicy, and knew everything about us. It was the first time we'd ever seen a brand book, which is the DNA of a brand in words and images. We looked at one he made for the launch of Russian Standard's Imperia vodka and it was staggering. Emphasizing the luxury vodka's authentic Russian heritage (it is distilled and bottled in Russia, unlike its chief competitor, Stolichnaya, which was bottled in Latvia at the time), he positioned Imperia alongside Russian icons like ballet dancer Mikhail Baryshnikov and fashion model Natalia Vodianova. Everything in the book was elegant, bold, and red, with women at the opera in red gowns, holding red bottles. It was an amazingly impactful presentation. Going from our crazy, self-styled Ellen von Unwerth shoot to these Madison Avenue pros, we knew they were the real deal.

It turned out our Trey Laird was Trey Laird.

Trey assigned Robert Lussier to be our project manager. When he and his team came out to visit our filthy, crazy office in Pacoima, they could not believe the Romper Room they were walking into. They were used to Seventh Avenue companies like Gap and Donna Karan. And for all our office renovations, we were still the circus of Juicy. And not Barnum & Bailey—more like a flea circus. We had a candy jar full of Rue de Pacoima notepads on the front desk and rainbow sand candles with everyone's names spelled on them at every workstation. And of course, our first question for him was, "Can you make an ad to fit a billboard?" Genius.

In preparation for the meeting, Robert had asked us to

put together some tear sheets and brainstorm the kinds of things we dream about. It wasn't unlike way back in the beginning when we'd brainstormed ideas to name our company, only now our aesthetic universe had grown even bigger. Some of the things we came up with were Marie Antoinette with a tower of cotton candy piled atop her head, Westies, 1950s debutantes, skater boys, *Charlie and the Chocolate Factory*, cake stands and jars of candy, Siouxsie and the Banshees, punk rock, and on and on.

Robert smiled and said, "Well, that's easy. That's Tim Walker." He handed us a book of photographs by the British fashion photographer, who has a vision so fairy-tale fantastical, he thinks nothing of coaxing a lion into a stately living room or creating a ten-foot-tall doll to chase a model through the forest to get the perfect shot. Walker got his start in fashion as an intern in the Condé Nast library, assembling an archive of Cecil Beaton's work. He photographed his first *Vogue* story at age twenty-five, and in the years following, his work appeared in nearly every glossy magazine, as well as the permanent collections of the Victoria & Albert Museum and the National Portrait Gallery in London. As we flipped through the pages, we got chills. We already had several of his photographs on our inspiration boards above our desks, including a famous image he took of a group of ice cream–colored Persian kittens after he had chalked their fur by hand. "That's our world! That's our flippin' world!" we told Robert. We just hadn't known until then that it was Tim Walker's world, too.

Robert and Tim understood us, which wasn't easy. Because as much as we liked fairy tales and flaxen-haired fashion dolls, our Juicy world wasn't about *The Princess and the Pea* and Barbie. It was elevated *Alice in Wonderland*-meets-*Willy Wonka*. It was a dreamscape, an acid trip, a fractured fairy tale. Now all we had to do was bring it to life.

Tim storyboarded our campaign with colored birds and Westie dogs. We said to him, "Marie Antoinette," and he came up with a drawn image of a girl with cotton-candy-pink hair, holding a giant perfume bottle, like Alice after she sinks (and shrinks) down the Rabbit Hole. The idea of cotton-candy hair led to the notion of using older ladies with their white hair dyed in cotton-candy colors. We loved the idea of having all ages represented in the campaign, because Juicy was for everyone. But it made for an interesting shoot, because those old ladies were anything but sweet.

The series of images, featuring a Marie Antoinette–like model, glam grannies, and a tattooed skater boy, turned out incredibly well. Tim's sense of color was so fairy-tale surreal, the images jumped off the page. He elevated our brand to the highest of the high. He didn't dumb it down or treat it like baby-land. Tim's a kindred spirit, intelligent and soulful but whimsical, and he lives his photographs. We collaborated with him and his partner, the stylist Jacob Kjeldgaard, many more times after that, and they have since become close personal friends of ours.

The Juicy Couture fragrance campaign ran in the all-important September issue of *Vogue* magazine, along with a story about our fragrance. It couldn't have been more perfect. On the cover was Kirsten Dunst, in a towering white cotton candy–like wig, dressed for her role as Marie Antoinette in the Sofia Coppola film that was to be released the following month. Talk about worlds colliding! Eau de Couture was off to a great start.

Our New York office suggested we have our fragrance launch party in the Hamptons, and we agreed, against our better judgment. The Hamptons was a place we had no connection to, but it was close to all the New York–based media. They also put us together with a high-profile New York–based party planner, who found the estate we rented and planned our event.

The party was scheduled for September 2, 2006, in Water Mill, New York. It was the same weekend the MTV Video Music Awards were being held in New York City, which was our first mistake. Every celebrity on the planet was going to be there, including the Durans, who were in the studio with Justin Timberlake and Timbaland. If we'd had the party in the city, they probably all would have come.

Another clue we'd messed up? We ran into the socialite Cornelia Guest at Barneys New York, and when we asked her to come, her response was, "You can't have a party in the Hamptons then. Nobody is going to be in town." Still, we thought they'd come for us, just like they had to all of our other parties from the launch of Juicy Jeans onward.

Well they didn't. At the party, our big guests of honor

were the Flying Tomato, Shaun White—and Hurricane Ernesto.

The storm was moving fast up the East Coast, getting closer every minute. We walked the red carpet, lanterns swaying perilously above us, with our dresses blowing up to our ears. It was a bad scene. The only thing to do was hide in the Andy Gump porta potty and get drunk.

After we'd had a few, a *Women's Wear Daily* reporter cornered us. "What does the fragrance smell like?" he asked. "Like money, motherfucker!" Pam said. It was time to go. We hightailed it back to the city that night, but not before we made the limo drive through McDonald's so we could get twenty bags of French fries.

A few weeks later, we returned to New York to make a personal appearance at Bloomingdale's Fifty-Ninth Street store for the launch of our fragrance. And that was a pick-me-up if ever there was one. There was a line around the block when we arrived, and we signed T-shirts and kissed dogs for hours.

Afterward, we took a taxi to Forty-Second Street, stepped out onto the sidewalk, looked up, and broke down. There, nestled into the New York skyline, was our first Times Square billboard, with our very own hundred-foot-tall cotton candy–haired queen. Juicy Couture had made its mark.

Dos and Don'ts of Hands-on Branding

Every detail counts.

Do make personal choices about logos and packaging that have an autobiographical story behind them. It will give your brand more meaning.

Do develop visual signatures and design codes that can carry over from one product category or licensed product to the next.

Don't just do what's popular, do what is authentic to you and your brand. You don't win by following others.

Don't sacrifice quality. Your customers will notice.

Do team with like-minded individuals to expand your vision at retail, through advertising and events.

Don't be pushed into something that doesn't feel like you. You are your brand.

Chapter 12

Big Is the Killer of Cool

Between 2005 and 2010, we were on a roller coaster of highs and lows. We opened dozens of stores with addresses on the crème de la crème of the world's retail streets, launched follow-up fragrances and made more money than we'd ever dreamed of.

But, as they say on VH1's *Behind the Music*, backstage things were falling apart. A change in regime at Liz Claiborne, a deepening rift between our management office in New York and our creative office in LA, plus competition from other fashion brands, ill-conceived product extensions, and the shock of the 2008 recession were the perfect storm. It was the beginning of the end, although we didn't know it yet. We were still living in the glory and high on fumes.

One of the high points was the opening of our Rodeo Drive store, a crown jewel in our backyard of Beverly Hills. We hired Philip Johnson to be our visual guru, our vice president of store design and creative services. Philip studied under the master, Simon Doonan, at Barneys New York, and he helped make the Rodeo Drive boutique the pinnacle of Juicyness by taking inspiration from our houses.

Located between Brooks Brothers and Ralph Lauren, the store was our largest yet at five thousand square feet. The facade was like a Georgian Colonial home straight out of 1930s-era Beverly Hills. Inside, there was a stunning gold winding staircase, marble floors, and Jacobian-style molded ceilings. On the walls, we had vintage taxidermy animal heads wearing long eyelashes and strands of pearls. There were also old oil paintings painted graffiti style with Juicyisms such as "Viva la Juicy," and a surfboard that read "Dude, Where's My Couture?"

Elegant rococo-style chairs were embroidered with "Go Couture Yourself" and "Buy Me Stuff." There were larger-than-life-size pink plastic knights, G&P initial rugs, and personalized wallpaper. Upstairs, there was a billiards room with parquet herringbone floors, a leather couch, and a fireplace. It felt more like a home than a store.

The space was the physical embodiment of our personalities, and it stocked the whole Juicy world in its entirety, from menswear to baby and kids to accessories. We even had a wall of tracksuits with chunks of rainbow colors.

By then, we had also created a whole new category of

gifts, including diamond-ring key chains, gum-ball machines, and $25 charms packaged in gilt-edged jewelry boxes with our signature terry-cloth lining instead of velvet. At the cash register, where it's all about impulse buys, we sold "Smells Like Couture" tube socks, roll-on fragrance sticks, and underwear packaged like giant lollipops. Bold letters on the shopping bags read "Love G&P." It was all our memories of Hard Rock Café, Fiorruci, Biba, shopping in Japan, and going to Disneyland rolled into one. It was a Juicy emporium. Willy Wonka, eat your heart out.

On November 7, 2007, we threw our most epic party yet to celebrate the opening. It was Cirque du Juicy, and we were the ringleaders in top hats and gowns. Guests were greeted by stilt walkers and handsome shirtless boys with riding crops in their hands. Discordant violins were playing. And when you walked into the store, you could see circus people sitting on shelves up high, and towers of macarons. Everyone in Hollywood showed up, including Halle Berry, Christina Aguilera, Demi Moore, Molly Sims, Gwen Stefani, and more. They all wore Juicy and wore it proudly. The hometown girls had done good.

But things that were beyond our control were beginning to change. Not only had our mentor and ally Angela Ahrendts left Liz Claiborne, but our sugar daddy, Paul Charron, had left, too. In a corporation, when the regime changes it can be significant. You may not see eye to eye with the new management. There may be a clash of cultures. And if you're not on the same page, you have to remember why you went into business for yourself in the first place, and decide if it's still worth it to go on when you're working for someone else.

Liz Claiborne's new CEO, Bill McComb, did not come from a fashion background, but instead from Johnson & Johnson, where he oversaw brands like Tylenol and Motrin. After he took over in 2006, he came out with a few members of his staff for a meet and greet at our offices in Pacoima. We arranged to have an In-N-Out Burger truck outside as a welcome to LA, and organized a town hall meeting to introduce them to our employees. Everyone loaded up on Double Doubles then settled in to meet the new suits. They proceeded to lead a PowerPoint presentation full of numbers and equations about their vision for growing Juicy Couture, which went over like when the parents or teachers talk in the *Peanuts* cartoons. And twenty minutes into it, we looked around the darkened room, and half our people were asleep, no doubt having blissful In-N-Out dreams.

We took to the floor to try to revive everyone, dressed in our outfits for the day, which involved short skirts and silly princess crowns. We'd just had an incredible experience with the Make-A-Wish Foundation, working with a young girl whose dream was to meet the Juicys and design with them. It was so special to know that we could impact someone like that. And we wanted to share it with our employees. They not only perked up, they started cheering and clapping. We had upstaged our new bosses, and they were not amused. Clearly, we were back to the drawing board with the Juicy-corporate mind meld. And we could have used something stronger than Bill's Tylenol at that moment.

Not only did Bill have a different style of communicating, he had a different outlook for the business, too. Where Paul had been focused on acquisitions, adding brands like Juicy to the Liz Claiborne fold, and consolidating operational efforts, such as marketing and licensing, under the control of the parent company, Bill had a different strategy. He whittled down the number of brands, closing some and selling others, to focus more attention on four "power brands" with the most potential for growth. Those brands were Lucky Brand, Kate Spade, Mexx, and Juicy Couture.

Bill had organizational changes in mind, too. He wanted each brand to be autonomous, with its own operational structure. And that meant restructuring the leadership. Instead of copresidents, he wanted us to be co–creative directors. We needed to hire a new president to run Juicy, and he gave us the two candidates to choose from. Edgar Huber was the winner, another nonfashion person, with a background at L'Oréal.

When it was all explained to us, we assumed Edgar would be headquartered in Los Angeles and would act as a bridge between our office and management in New York. We also assumed we would continue to have input in our budget and staffing. We were wrong about all of that. Not only did Edgar never move west, but as the months went on, we felt more and more left out of key decisions. We didn't have an open forum to bear our grievances, and couldn't get money for initiatives to grow our brand. We were like Gilligan stranded in Los Angeles.

We were facing challenges on the product side, too.

The most difficult thing about having a brand like Juicy, which becomes so successful and so iconic, is that your customers are a huge wave that pushes you in a certain direction. In fashion, if you become mainstream you're not cool anymore, so it's a constant balancing act. We didn't start Juicy to be the thing teenagers die over. It was supposed to be casual luxury that was aspirational. But increasingly, that wasn't the case.

Our licensed products, including fragrance, sunglasses, watches, and accessories, were selling really well, so well in fact that the market was starting to get flooded with Juicy. There were too many tracksuits, too. You'd walk into a department store and see racks of them as far as the eye could see. Then racks of knockoff Juicy tracksuits next to those. You cannot stay on top when you're a whole floor at Bloomingdale's Fifty-Ninth Street flagship. Because in fashion, big is the killer of cool. Keeping people hungry is the key.

We had started to feel the chill back in April 2005, when a shopping columnist at *The New York Times* wrote a review of our Las Vegas store. "I think of two things when I hear the words 'Juicy Couture.' One, the cashmere sweatsuit. And two, over. So over. As over as Ugg boots worn on a hot California day with a denim miniskirt, fake-tan legs, and lips plumped with too much collagen. That over," she wrote.

Now, that was one person's opinion, and we went on to sell millions of tracksuits after that. But it put us on notice. We didn't want to be labeled a one-trick pony.

We were also feeling competition from a new group of advanced contemporary designers, led by Tory Burch, who were making clothing at accessible price points that looked more aspirational than Juicy. We had a meeting with Saks Fifth Avenue president Ron Frasch, who suggested we come up with something new to hit that market. Our answer was Couture Couture, a twenty-piece designer collection launched in October 2005 to appeal to an older, more fashion-forward customer.

It had higher prices ($500 to $4,000 versus Juicy's $180 average price point), and more dressed-up pieces in luxe fabrications, including lace skirts, jewel-encrusted dresses, and a silver linen pantsuit. But it wasn't differentiated enough from Juicy to be a success. A woman couldn't go into a Juicy store and make logical sense out of spending $800 on a pair of trousers from Couture Couture that she could get for $250 from Juicy.

When you are adding product categories, which you have to do to grow and stay current, you need to be thoughtful. There's nothing wrong with adding another label. Michael Kors and Ralph Lauren built their businesses by doing that. But Couture Couture didn't turn out to be the right label. It was too price-prohibitive and said the wrong thing.

Our instinct was right, though. The tracksuit had gone from casual luxury to glitzed-out, logoed tourist attraction. We needed to move on. But the powers that be wouldn't let us. They just wanted to keep anniversary-ing what was selling, which is the lowest common denominator. It was all about the cheapest, easiest, opening price point, souvenir T-shirt and tracksuit. All of a sudden, we found ourselves doing that and only that. And that's how a brand dies.

In meetings, when we'd be picking colors and logos, they didn't want to listen to what we had to say about trying something new. They'd say, "It's going to be fuchsia because that's our big seller. It's going to have sequins because that's our big seller."

And that's the absolute difference between corporate and entrepreneurial mind-sets. A suit looks at reports. If reports say *this* is selling, it's design more of *this*. The entrepreneur says, "I feel a change coming around the bend, we need to get out of *this* and start getting into *that*. *That* is the new trend." The corporate mind-set won't do that unless they take a survey of one hundred people. The entrepreneur says, "It doesn't matter what they say they want because they don't know they want it yet."

A good management team is able to meld what the entrepreneurial mind says is coming next and what the corporate mind says is working now. One is gut and the other is report. But when we should have been thinking about the future, we were just staying in the present. When we desperately should have been hiring teams to elevate our product, we couldn't.

The one person we were able to hire was Frances Pennington, our wonderful global head of marketing and PR. She brought fresh energy and radically great ideas (plus a pixie haircut we thought was the coolest). She was what we needed for every department: that kind of next-level talent. If only we had been so lucky.

In 2008, when the recession hit, it hit the apparel industry particularly hard. Liz Claiborne (like many companies) was suffering losses. We were under a hiring freeze, and our management was doing anything and everything to try to get sales back up. One day, someone came out from New York and told us that one of our stores wanted a line of yoga clothes. And the next day, Juicy was developing a yoga wear line called Down Dog Couture with the same exhausted, overtaxed team. How could we possibly take on a new label when we barely had enough people to design Juicy? Our team was woefully small compared to most businesses our size.

But even if we tried to say no to ideas from management, sometimes they listened, and sometimes they didn't. But most times, they didn't even ask. Are you beginning to get the picture?

We were being forced to spread ourselves way too thin at a time when the core women's product was already on shaky ground. We should have worked on the foundation, made it aspirational again, before layering on other brand categories. Don't add a second story when your house is falling down!

But we didn't have enough control to turn it around. We couldn't say, "We're not doing yoga," or "We're not selling this many tracksuits to you because it's going to cheapen the brand," or "If you don't buy our shoes and our Couture Couture collection, you're not getting Juicy at all." We couldn't pull back when we needed to, because our management and our creative teams were at odds.

Management was obsessed with margins, so the merchandisers would come out from New York and make the designers change details on the clothing so the profit margins on a sale would be higher. Executives would breeze into town and say, "Guess what, we just sold your sourcing; you're transitioning in three months." (In fashion speak, sourcing is the practice of contracting suppliers and manufacturers to produce your goods overseas.) And we'd say, "But it's going to kill our quality!" (We thought we had a choice.) And they'd respond, "It's done."

When the first batch of clothing came in after our sourcing was sold, logos were printed so poorly, they looked like damages, and the velour felt like sandpaper. It was horrible. Juicy was all about fit, fabric, and color. And this was something else. Our world had changed. By the time we didn't want to wear the clothes or the bags, that was truly the end.

We tried again to reinvent and elevate with a line called

Bird, launched in 2009, which was priced at about 30 percent more than Juicy. It was launched to go in our new Fifth Avenue store, as a marketing vehicle, and it was a success, probably because there were no logos on it. But by then, it was too late.

Liz Claiborne had seen three straight years of earnings declines. And according to the first-quarter financials reported in May 2009, Juicy Couture's comparable store sales were down 22 percent from the same time in 2008. The suits blamed us. Juicy Couture wasn't the golden child anymore. The new growth vehicle was Kate Spade. We went from being respected and loved and feeling like our opinions mattered, to feeling like we were lame ducks and they were smoking us out.

Our employees could feel the tension, too. Juicy was no longer a fun place to be. We still brought our dogs to work but even they hated it there. The culture was different. The Halloween pageants were long gone. And so were the intercom practical jokes. When Janey told us she was leaving, we thought she was kidding. She'd been with us since the beginning. But she was beyond wiped out. Everyone was. At her going-away party, there was not a dry eye in the building. She'd touched so many people.

At Liz Claiborne, people were being fired left and right. And Juicy was not left out. There were pink slips landing every day. Instead of a supportive environment, there were people going behind closed doors telling stories and trying to save their own skins. Our new president had new rules, too.

One day, our office manager came in to our office, crying. She had gotten a company memo saying she could no longer feed the feral cats outside. "What is the poor cat family going to do?" she asked. Food for that cat family had been part of our company budget since year one. We told her, "Of course you can still feed the cats."

But the message was deeper: Our philosophy had always been, mix it with love, and the world feels that love in a T-shirt. When you can't feed the cats in the parking lot anymore, where's the love? The culture was smashed to smithereens. And it was taking its toll. Everyone was overworked. The design team was there until eleven P.M. every night. Our head of PR landed in the hospital because of the stress. How can anyone be productive in a culture of fear?

We called our old boss Paul Charron and asked him if we'd done something wrong. He said, "No, the only thing you did wrong is that you forgot you sold your company. It isn't yours anymore." At least he and Angela had allowed us to believe it still was. To weather a storm like the recession of 2008, you better have a general who is on your side, and every single thing you do better be for the good of the brand. We had the opposite.

To add injury to insult, Pam broke her ankle in several places while she was skimboarding, an accident that landed her in surgery and then in bed for six weeks. While Gela was dodging punches at work, Pam was at home with a frozen contraption on her leg. We're never good when we're apart, so we'd spend hours on the phone every day boohooing. We agreed that Juicy was no longer our vision. It was not casual luxury and it was not a fun, loving place to work. We'd stayed at the party way too long. Our contracts were up and we didn't want to renew them. It was time to let go.

Back in Pacoima a month later, we didn't even clean out our desks and makeup drawers or grab the pictures off our brag wall. We just took the lucky Santeria candle we had bought in downtown LA all those years ago and drove into the sunset with the wheels already spinning in our heads about what was next.

We couldn't believe we were leaving this thing we'd created. But the people you work with can change everything. We had a difference in opinion with management, and for all the fallout that's ensued, we're very proud that we've taken the high road.

In the end, it wasn't about the money or the deal; it was about our beautiful baby, our brand. Our contract was up, but we still had to look at the Juicy Couture ads and windows. And it was painful.

Even today, we look at Juicy and feel like we could turn it around. Remember when new Coke came in and it was the biggest bomb ever? We still feel like old Coke could come back and kill it.

Chapter 13

Do It All Over Again

After we left our baby, the company we founded, we were dazed and confused. It had all happened so fast and we felt displaced. We purged everything with a Juicy label from our closets. We couldn't bear to look at it. (Though in the end, we just ended up screwing ourselves, because we didn't have any comfy clothes to wear!)

Gela took Mickey Drexler's approach. The CEO, who famously made Gap cool in the 1990s, and was abruptly fired in 2002, never looked in a Gap window or shopped in a Gap store again. (He went on to get redemption at J.Crew, which he has built into one of the biggest retail success stories of the new millennium.)

For Pam, forgetting about Juicy was more difficult. She spent every weekend at the beach, eating lunch at Malibu Kitchen, right next door to the Juicy store at Malibu Country Mart. Walking by that store window, it was like she was looking at a child she knew but didn't recognize. She wanted desperately to walk in and restyle the mannequins. If only they paired that cashmere sweater with those pants, it would look amazing, she thought. And where did the charm table go?

Where Juicy cashmere used to be the uniform in Malibu, nobody was wearing it anymore. And all the Juicy pink shopping bags had vanished. No one was buying it, either. It was heartbreaking.

So many people said to us, You played it so well. You got out at just the right time and made so much money. Why don't you just ride into the sunset? But those are suits, not entrepreneurs, and they don't get the burn.

A true entrepreneur understands the single-mindedness that borders on being obsessive-compulsive. And that the work of an entrepreneur doesn't end with any single business. It's on to the next. We like making clothes, creating a world, and building a brand almost more than we like anything. We have to be in the fashion business. We can't help it; it's all we know how to do.

We felt like racehorses champing at the bit to get out of the gate and into the race again. But we had a noncompete clause in our Juicy contract that stipulated we could not work in the fashion industry until July 31, 2011.

We tried to move on and focus on other things. Gela retreated to her house in the English countryside. After so many years of working, she had fantasies of learning how to cook, garden, and speak French fluently. What she did instead was go to every vintage fair in the British Isles and start making boards of steampunk looks. She played with clothes all day long.

Meanwhile in LA, Pam thought about building a painting studio in her backyard, doing photography again, and taking all those long lunches with friends that she never had a chance to take during years of eating at her desk in Pacoima. Instead, she browsed vintage on Etsy and eBay until the wee hours, and holed up in her basement going through old magazines and fashion and art books, and adding to her mental inspiration board.

Back together again in LA during the summer of 2011, we were still full of anxiety and sadness. We took long walks every day. For four or five hours, we'd walk and walk and walk and walk and talk. We did that for a long time, meditating, healing, and thinking about what we were going to do next. Eventually, instead of being hurt, we realized we were still the luckiest girls in the world. It wasn't anything we did; there were just circumstances beyond our control that made it impossible for us to continue at Juicy.

The age-old question about women and the workplace is, Can you have it all? The answer is no. When you're driven, something in your life does always suffer. Pam had guilt about working so much when her son, Noah, was a baby. When she was with him, she was thinking about work, and when she was working, she was thinking about him. On the weekends, she'd try to overcompensate. But something always suffers. And it's usually the woman!

For Gela to work in LA with Pam, she had to give up a lot, since John lived most of the time in England. In two months, sometimes Gela would only see him for two days. She also had two children and a stepdaughter to nurture while she was working and traveling around the world.

And yet, when we didn't have work, we went crazy. When you're a creative person, you have to create. Retirement isn't part of that mentality. The mentality is, What is inspiring you next?

While we were halfway around the world from each other, we both happened to watch the 1970 film *Performance* featuring Italian actress and rock 'n' roll muse Anita Pallenberg. We watched the same movie in the same two days without even knowing it! Then, when we were chatting during one of our daily phone calls, Pam said, "I'm really feeling Anita . . ." Gela finished the sentence: "Pallenberg? Me too!"

We took it as a sign. Pallenberg was a reminder of what we started loving about fashion all those years ago when we were thrifting and vintageing for quirky finds. We had been doing casual luxury at Juicy for years, a uniform, and we wanted to take a different road, something more free-spirited and individual. That's how our next label, Skaist Taylor, was born.

At 12:01 A.M. on July 31, 2011, the minute our noncompete was over, we whipped out the tequila, did a dance, and said a prayer for Juicy. Then we started putting together our new collection. We were ready to put the past behind us. We started creating looks and a SKU plan, figuring out how many dresses and pants we'd have. The concept was "California eccentric," with oversize fur coats, metallic minidresses, embroidered peasant blouses, and skintight leather pants.

We wanted to have a runway show to launch our collection at New York Fashion Week in February, which was something we'd never done before at Juicy. But us being us, we'd never just do a boring, straight, seated show. We wanted it to be a happening—very personal, fun, and LA.

We tapped the amazing creative team of Patrick Kinmonth and Antonio Monfreda, who had worked on Valentino's forty-five-year extravaganza in Rome, to make a short film as a backdrop for the show featuring our model and muse Theodora Richards, who is the daughter of Patti Hansen and Rolling Stones guitarist Keith Richards. We filmed her running through the California pines in the forest behind Pam's house. And we unearthed a venue that had never been used for fashion: the parking garage underneath Lincoln Center, which is the hub of New York Fashion Week.

Our production crew was still towing cars at three A.M., but everything went off without a hitch. The film projections on the walls transformed the garage into an illusionary maze of trees from floor to ceiling, and a sound track of

California-inspired tunes curated by John added to the ambiance. We showed the collection in short presentations on a runway, with people gathered around to see. The clothes were a combination of luxurious knits, furs, suits, and dresses. It was like a walk through our closets. And to come out of that dark moment after Juicy and collaborate again was so gratifying.

We had a ton of RSVPs, so we knew people were interested in what we were doing. But we were worried what they would think. All of our friends from the industry came, including Neiman Marcus fashion director Ken Downing, Net-a-Porter.com founder Natalie Massenet, Bloomingdale's vice-chairman and general merchandise manager Frank Doroff, and Bergdorf Goodman fashion director Linda Fargo. It was a kick to see them all, and *Vogue* editor in chief Anna Wintour, in our underground Cali clubhouse. And when Hamish Bowles, international editor at large at *Vogue*, came backstage and starting making notes, we really knew we were on to something. *Harper's Bazaar*'s Glenda Bailey was front and center, too, cheering us on like she always has.

The next day, when we picked up *Women's Wear Daily* from in front of our hotel-room door, there was a picture of us on the cover with a headline that read "We're back!" We fell to our knees and started crying.

The collection was a critical success. It landed in the windows of Maxfield, LA's edgiest, coolest high-fashion store, and Bergdorf Goodman in New York. Neiman Marcus, Nordstrom, Harrods, and Harvey Nichols also bought it in limited quantities. We were featured in *Bazaar*, *WWD*, and the *Los Angeles Times*, and we had some nice celebrity hits. January Jones wore our fur-trimmed band jacket right away, Kim Kardashian wore our leather pants, and Khloe Kardashian wore our turtleneck minidress.

At that time, we just wanted to make incredible pieces. We weren't thinking about anniversarying things and sell-throughs. We weren't thinking about business at all, we were just thinking about beauty. But we realized after a few seasons, you can't survive on beauty.

Skaist Taylor was expensive, with prices in the $600 to $2,000 range. As a business, it was very small and precious compared to where we came from. It was a great jumping-off point, but we wanted something bigger. Plus, we didn't follow our own advice in this book, because the name was tricky. It didn't stick in people's heads because they couldn't pronounce Skaist (it's *Sky-ste*).

Not that we regret it for a minute. It was a cleansing experience. By the end at Juicy, we were basically designing by numbers, and we had to do something that was the total opposite of that corporate mentality.

But after purging all of the Juicy from our closets, we were left with a void. We wanted to make clothes people would wear every day, that feel like a second skin, not clothes that you wear once or twice. We had been nervous about going near casual luxury again. But it's home. That's Pam and Gela.

We were afraid to say it out loud, but we always knew we wanted Juicy back. And in 2013, we started on a journey to try and get it.

Early in the year, we got an e-mail from Peter Comisar, an investment banker with the LA-based firm Guggenheim Partners, whom we have known for years and counted as a trusted advisor. Peter focuses on mergers and acquisitions, and has advised many corporations, brands, and retailers. He had become aware that Fifth & Pacific (the company changed its name after CEO Bill McComb sold the rights to the Liz Claiborne brand to JCPenney) was looking to sell the Juicy Couture business, and Peter saw an opportunity.

It was common knowledge that Juicy was not doing well. Where it was once a $1 billion brand with global resonance, the wheels were coming off the train when it came to product and execution. Even after management brought in a string of new creative directors, no one could restore the brand to its glory days. In 2012, Juicy reported a 62 percent drop in earnings to $24.6 million. And Juicy's sales fell 6 percent to $499 million. Still, we thought we could revive it. Like old Coke coming back in and killing it, remember? But first, we had to know what we were dealing with.

At the time, Juicy had more than three hundred stores worldwide, including outlets. But the last time we'd been into one of them was when the brand was in its glory days. So we put on dark glasses and hats, and headed out *Mod*

Squad like on an expedition to the Juicy store on Rodeo Drive.

When we stepped in the front door, it was like we had amnesia. We had no idea where we were. The G&Ps were gone from the carpets and chairs, the banisters, and fixtures. Not only had our names been whitewashed from the fairy tale on the wall, the whole fairy tale had been removed. The candy, the fun, and the whimsy was gone. The clothing didn't look familiar, either; the slogans on the T-shirts were sly and sexual, like something you'd see for sale on Hollywood Boulevard. It was crazy how much had changed in so little time. We didn't see ourselves anywhere in the brand.

Even though Juicy was the *Titanic* (all they needed were the violins playing), we felt like we were the lifeboat. We wanted to buy the business and make it relevant again. But the valuation was a couple hundred million dollars or more, and we weren't in a place where we wanted to do a deal like that by ourselves. Plus, our skill is in design, marketing, and product, not in finance. That's where Guggenheim came in. Peter offered to be our strategic partner and help us raise money to buy back the business.

We worked together to create a package for potential investors, laying out what we would do differently and how we would revive the brand. Then we went to New York to have preliminary meetings with private equity firms to gauge their interest. Many of them thought Juicy was a falling knife, a financial term meaning that while the price of the stock seemed attractive, it was too good to be true, and

Juicy was actually overvalued relative to its prospects. Other potential players we met were never allowed to join the bidding process, because Fifth & Pacific kept the discussions very narrow.

It's true that it was going to be a difficult turnaround, because what the brand stood for had changed so dramatically. Peter told us our value in the process was going to be in convincing a financial partner we had the goods to make Juicy relevant again. But even he was skeptical, telling us candidly that his wife would never be caught dead in a Juicy tracksuit. Instead of giving up, he challenged us. "If you want to do this deal, show us what the product is going to look like," he said.

So we did what we do best—we put together a collection. We had to see if we would wear and want Juicy again.

We called in Annie Tran, a designer who had started with us at Juicy, and was now freelance. We had to start tapping into the casual luxury side of ourselves again. That meant T-shirts, sweats, the casual clothes you live in.

We designed a high-quality terry-cloth zip-back jacket, terry pants with ribbed cuffs that could be pushed up to the knee and worn with gladiator sandals, vintage-inspired sundresses and rompers, a python biker jacket, and leather shorts. The designing and merchandising, it all came so easily, which is how it should be. We were figuring out what a new generation of Juicy women would want to wear now.

Once Peter and his associates at Guggenheim saw the collection, they upped the ante. Instead of just being a strategic partner, they wanted to be our financial partner, too. They offered to put up the capital we needed to buy Juicy from Fifth & Pacific and make an ongoing investment in the infrastructure, design, and resources to help us turn the brand around.

So in May, together with Guggenheim, we made a proposal to buy Juicy for $200 million, an offer that was later increased to $250 million. Our hope was to keep the retail stores open, execute a turnaround in product, and focus on keeping Juicy elevated as the global affordable luxury brand it had been in its heyday.

But we were told it wasn't enough. We didn't really believe that, but we made the decision to back away from the process. We just couldn't see paying any more than $250 million given the investment that was going to be required in the long run to return the brand to its former stature.

The $196 million offer Fifth and Pacific ultimately accepted in October sold the intellectual property of Juicy Couture to a company called Authentic Brands Group, whose portfolio also includes TapouT, Marilyn Monroe, Judith Leiber, Adrienne Vittadini, and Taryn Rose. ABG subsequently made a deal to take Juicy to a more mass channel: Kohl's department stores.

When a brand is distressed, there are two forks in the road. Either you can fix the product and continue to have branded boutiques and sell at high-end department stores. Or you can do what's been done with brands such as Mossimo, Op, and now Juicy—take them to a new channel, where the price point and what the brand stands for will be very different than it was under the founders.

Juicy will be taking on a new life beginning in fall 2014. But we feel it could have been something much different.

We realized that if we couldn't get Juicy back, we weren't going to let that stop us. And that's how our current label, Pam & Gela, was born. In the summer of 2013, we took the new capsule collection we'd designed to our sales rep, Betsee Isenberg, in LA, who is the barometer of taste and all that's good, and only takes collections she thinks will turn into big businesses. She looked at the pieces and said, "This is it."

In September, we went with her to market in New York because we wanted to hear retailers' reactions for ourselves. We were nervous about launching another collection so soon, and under a different name. But Betsee said no one would care. And she was right. Nobody batted an eye. Everybody got it immediately. Because in the end, product is king. And the name Pam & Gela was queen!

We wrote a ton of business. Every department store picked up Pam & Gela, and so did hundreds of boutiques, including Intermix, Maxfield, and Shopbop.com. We showed the collection to Maya Singer at Style.com and got a great review. "The Pam & Gela girl is hanging out at the corner of Melrose and La Brea," she wrote. "It speaks to Skaist-Levy and Nash-Taylor's savvy that it's so easy to visualize her. Pam & Gela feels on-target." And our old pal Frank Doroff is building us a shop-in-shop at Bloomingdale's on Fifty-Ninth Street just like we did in the early days of Juicy.

When we started Juicy, we talked about designing a modern uniform, something that would fit well, be comfortable, and make your body look insane. Pam & Gela is the same philosophy of fit, fabric, and color, but updated for today, and for what we want to wear now.

It's a different kind of uniform of easy, casual pieces that are the building blocks of your wardrobe. A ruched jersey knee-length skirt has gathers that make your butt look amazing. A high-low-hem sweatshirt dips down in the back to cover what you want to cover, and has cozy, therapeutic thumbholes so you can pull the sleeves down over your hands. It's like fashion comfort food, with prices ranging from $115 for a T-shirt to $995 for a leather jacket.

We're working with 100 percent cotton fleece, which is pure luxury. Instead of looking at color as a crazy rainbow, we're looking at color the way we want to wear it now. It's more subtle, not like candy—blush pink instead of bubblegum and dusty sky blue instead of electric blue. And we are doing a portion of our manufacturing in Los Angeles again, because philosophically, it's the right thing to do for us and for the brand because it's who we are.

Another thing that is consistent? Juicy always had a sense of humor. And we still have a sense of humor. We designed a pair of sweatpants with the word "Duh" spelled out across the butt. We don't know if we'll sell them, but we think they are hysterical. We also have logo T-shirts that read "I'm not sorry." Because we're not ashamed of what we did at Juicy and we want to reference it every now and then. Wink, wink.

Fashion has changed a lot since we started Juicy in 1995. We'll always be remembered for taking the idea of athletic wear and turning it into fashion you could wear from carpool to dinner at Mr. Chow. Then brands like Lululemon came along after us, and now women wear actual workout clothes everywhere, which baffles us. They've taken it to another level. And now it's time to bring fashion back to the comfort equation.

So much of success is timing. If we'd started Pam & Gela right out of the gate, it probably wouldn't have worked. But people want this from us again. Because the truth is, there isn't a girl in the world who doesn't get dressed to go to the office every day and say, I just want to get home, rip off my clothes, and put on my sweats. We want everyone to have that feeling in their day-to-day wardrobe. Because when you are comfortable, you are happy. And that's good style.

Back in the late '90s, everyone (us included) was so label-conscious. There was no fast fashion back then. Today, when you say, I got this top at Zara, people think you scored. Fast fashion has cachet. Celebrities want to wear a Topshop jacket with a Prada skirt. H&M does collaborations with high-end labels like Marni and Isabel Marant. Women know how to shop high and low at the same time, and mix it all up in their wardrobes. They want it all. And they want it their way.

The new Pam & Gela world will be more clean and less produced. That feels right for right now. We have an idea for a store that has an organic, raw feel. We don't want something so static it can't change with our collections.

We've learned lessons, too, like don't run before you can walk. We want to do accessories, jewelry, and fragrance. But it's better to be mindful, and launch something new when you are 100 percent ready to do it the right way, not when you're so hot you think you can sell ice to Eskimos.

We are starting with another fairy-tale beginning, and we couldn't be more excited to do it all over again.

Once upon a time, there were two nice girls . . .

Love, Pam and Gela

Acknowledgments

Paul Charron, Angela Ahrendts, Frank Doroff, Michael Gould, Karen Katz, Ken Downing, Ron Frasch, Burt Tansky, Jim Gold, Linda Fargo, Terry Lundgren, Pete Nordstrom, Natalie Massenet, Glenda Bailey, Sally Singer, Hamish Bowles, Hal Rubenstein, Sasha Charnin-Morrison, Plum Sykes, Diane Merrick, Tracey Ross, John Eshaya, Ron Herman, Janey Lopaty, Elva Gonzalez, Vicki Goldshtein, Jan Matthey, Annie Tran, Ade Wood, Phillip Johnson, Laura Anthony, Gerard Dislaire, Lisa Metcalfe, Diana Duran, Kwila Lee, Lisa Shaller-Goldberg, Joanne Fiske, Amanda Cannon, Jillian Kirk, Katharine Tierney, Lara Shriftman, Elizabeth Harrison, Sunny Cha, Angela Torti, Christina Miller, Mike Scarpa, Trudy Sullivan, Tracy Burnett, Sandra Bernhard, Tim McMullan, Peter Morton, Robert Lussier, Trey Laird, Arianne Phillips,

Jessica Paster, Andrea Lieberman, Rachel Zoe, Tim Walker, Jacob Kjeldgaard, Frances Pennington, Karla Otto, Meghan Murray-Merriman, Debra Thom, Art Spiro, Arnold Ephraums, Susan Kellog, Jill Granoff, Bonnie Brooks, 1927 Ltd., Imaginex Group, Jay Mangel, SAGE Group, Peter Comisar, Guggenheim Partners, Duran Duran, Klauber Brothers, Inc., Almore Dye House, Shara-Tex Inc., Eclat Textile, Zabin Industries, Travis Nash, Ashley Agedah, Chris Turner, Taylor Babaian, Adam Tschorn, Lauren Marino, Lupe Hernandez, Elizabeth "Bit" Harris, Lisa Rodrigues, Morgan Gilman, Amy Licata, Tink, Dan, Bubba, Baby, Fish, Chips, Mary, Bob, Violet, Johnny Rocket, Sid Vicious, Etiquette, and all the Juicy girls everywhere.